LIVING OUT LOUD

LETTING YOUR LOVE FOR GOD
FLOW INTO YOUR EVERYDAY LANGUAGE

LIVING

(((OUT)))

LOUD

KEVIN KING

WITH CHRISTINE DANIELS

Visit Tyndale online at tyndale.com.

Tyndale and Tyndale's quill logo are registered trademarks of Tyndale House Ministries.

Living Out Loud: Letting Your Love for God Flow into Your Everyday Language

For information about special discounts for bulk purchases, please contact Tyndale House Publishers at csresponse@tyndale.com, or call 1-855-277-9400.

Library of Congress Cataloging-in-Publication Data

A catalog record for this book is available from the Library of Congress.

ISBN 978-1-4964-9002-5

Printed in the United States of America

30	29	28	27	26	25	24
7	6	5	4	3	2	1

CONTENTS

FOREWORD

IN THE 1950s, as evangelicalism began its ascent as a cultural force, *evangelism*—the act of communicating the gospel—was mostly described as a *program*. It often took the form of a crusade, a presentation, or a set of steps. It always concluded with a prayer. It assumed some basic truths about a person's worldview. It was something you went out and *did*.

This view of evangelism was so widespread within the church that now, some seventy years later, we continue to struggle with it. A couple of cultural shifts have occurred since then, but the idea that we are still "doing evangelism" persists in the hearts and minds of many believers. Even when we know better, it is difficult to divorce ourselves from this way of thinking.

These cultural shifts have, of course, landed the world in a place further removed from the truths we know must be communicated. Jesus commanded us to take the gospel to the whole world, proclaiming God's Kingdom to all. So there's no avoiding it. To be obedient demands that we "do evangelism."

The problem is not in the *doing*, but in the myriad of assumptions that inhabit the word *do*.

When I worked cross-culturally in a war-torn region of the world, I wondered how the gospel message could ever be communicated. The suffering, the suspicion of others, and the hatred that lingered were seemingly insurmountable. As our team struggled to figure out how to "do evangelism," God was at work. He took the hatred that was all around us and turned it on its head. In a country with vast numbers of soul-wounded people, God put together a small church that had people from all sides. They were friends in a sea of enemies. They loved each other, very imperfectly but powerfully, in a place that knew little love. This was the power of the gospel in that context. The contrast that came with the culture around that little church was how God "did evangelism" among those people.

The manner of outreach is easier when the environment is totally different. We don't tend to take our cultural assumptions in with us. We make room for God to work in ways that we find hard to do in our own environments. Can we make room in our everyday lives as we seek to invite others into the Kingdom? It is time for us to wake up from this illusion we have about evangelism as a *project*.

I have been a friend and observer of International Project for some time. This is a ministry that doesn't "do" evangelism. They *live* it. Kevin and Christine are a part of a group of people that have tackled some of the biggest challenges in urban ministry by helping God's people step into a transformed way of life.

As I write this foreword, I am in Cairo, Egypt, one of the world's great cities. The issues presented by this culture are very different from those in New York City, or my hometown of Orlando, Florida. Yet, the same human need for a relationship with Jesus exists. Evangelism that addresses these universal human needs is not constrained by culture.

Yet, as you read this book, I suggest that you envision your own neighborhood and ask yourself how these principles would play out in that context. What you will find is that this book is not a how-to manual of techniques and strategies to follow, or a list of "tools" to use. Instead, Kevin and Christine highlight relationships, conversations, acts of service, and ways to love others as we live and speak as spiritual people.

In these pages, you will encounter a Kingdom worldview that sees people where they are and seeks to love them into God's family.

Ted Esler
President, Missio Nexus
Cairo, Egypt

INTRODUCTION

WE'VE BOTH BEEN CHRISTIANS for more than thirty years. Throughout our journeys of following Jesus, we've seen the church (ourselves included) neglect the call to talk about God. And we've experienced how lifeless a walk with Jesus can be when we miss out on the adventure of obeying him. We've also seen the fruit that comes from speaking about God. And we've experienced how fun it is to walk with Jesus when he uses our obedience to advance his Kingdom.

Our friendship has grown as our families have connected over these shared convictions and passions. So as God stirred these desires in us more and more, and as people we talked with seemed to be encouraged by them, we decided to write a book together. It turned out to be a bit tricky. Do we write as *we*, or do we take the time to make sure you know which one of us is speaking at every turn? Do we alternate writing chapters or go half-and-half down the middle? Every approach seemed to hinder the way our thoughts flowed onto the page. Ultimately, we decided that it would be best to write the book from a personal perspective, even if you might not always know which *I* is which (except when we reference our spouses, which kind of gives it away).

We think that's okay. Maybe even a strength. We come from different places, with different ideas, experiences, and stories to tell. We're from different states, generations, and denominations. But we both agree with what we've written, and we hope you find it compelling, convicting, and encouraging as we share what God has done.

But before we go incognito, we want to give you a bit of our background as individuals. Perhaps it will help you recognize our voices throughout the book.

KEVIN

I went to a Catholic high school. My family wasn't religious or anything, but it was the best educational option at the time. During my junior year, I was required to take religion classes, and they got me questioning some things. I started reading the Bible so I could debate my teachers. I'd read a section, form an argument, and then bring it up in class. Sections turned into chapters, which turned into books, and all the while God was turning my heart and mind upside down.

After a few months of this, I began searching for someone apart from school who could help me understand Jesus better. My cousin recommended that I talk to her father-in-law, and he explained the gospel to me more fully. A couple of months later, I visited a local nondenominational church and made a profession of faith to follow Jesus, and by spring of my junior year, I had decided to get baptized.

When I went back to school that fall, I started talking about my new faith in Jesus. It wasn't long before I was called to the principal's office and warned that if I continued to talk to others about my beliefs, they were going to ask me to leave the school. I didn't stop. After two more meetings with the principal—and even though a group of teachers and priests actually circulated a petition to have me expelled—I was allowed to complete the final months of my senior year. Those encounters had a big impact on me, and I became even more passionate and tenacious about sharing the gospel with others.

After graduation, I went to a Bible college and took evangelism classes. I memorized and practiced gospel presentations. I went up to people cold turkey and shared with them. I really had a heart to see lost people find Jesus, but I didn't have a whole lot of regard for their needs in a particular moment. And though I still believe there is value in learning a clear gospel presentation and setting aside time to share it with people, it started becoming more and more clear that my idea of evangelism was missing something. When I decided to go out witnessing, I went with courage and gumption. But most of the time, the gospel wasn't coming up in natural ways. Unless I had already planned to share the gospel with someone, spiritual things weren't part of the conversation.

Over many years, God shifted my ideas about how, why, when, and where to engage people spiritually. In 1998, my wife and I moved to New York City to focus on ministering to unreached people groups. In 2010 (through International Project), I started a training program called Equip, focused on helping cross-cultural church planters develop their ministry skills. It soon became clear that most ministry skills are *universal*, meaning they work in any culture, with any people group, and for any age. Another important lesson I learned is that knowing how and when to turn up your spiritual volume in a natural, organic way is the most necessary and important skill for ongoing, consistent spiritual engagement that produces good fruit.

Maybe you're like I was, turning your spirituality on and off at any given moment. Maybe you enter conversations with evangelistic fervor or no evangelism at all. And maybe you sense something is missing from all your interactions. If your journey is anything like mine has been, I'm confident I can help you. There were many times when I didn't speak up, and I regret those times. There were also many times when I did speak up but left discouraged by the lack of response, feeling that there must be a better way. This struggle is what ultimately led me to write this book. It's about letting your love for God flow naturally into your everyday language. It's about the freedom we have, as spiritual people, to bring spiritual things into our daily conversations. And as we speak, whether it's comfortable or awkward in a given situation, God will use our words in incredible ways to draw people to himself.

CHRISTINE

It was an early morning flight, and I was really tired. My desire to fall asleep, coupled with my motion sickness, rendered me virtually useless from takeoff to landing. I remember ignoring the nagging guilt I felt for not taking the opportunity to share the gospel with the captive audience alongside me in row 17. I grew up in a church where trying to convert people on airplanes was deeply ingrained in the culture. By not doing my part, I was being a "bad" Christian.

As I was drifting off under the influence of Dramamine, I heard the woman in 15F strike up a conversation with the man next to her. They talked about the weather and their kids and where their travels were taking them. To the average eavesdropper, this conversation would be boring, but I was invested in it because I knew where it was headed. The woman in 15F was a friend of mine from church, and she was a "good" Christian.

Right after the topic of local restaurants died down, my friend turned to her seatmate and asked the question I knew she'd been waiting to ask: "Where do you think you'll go when you die?"

The man was obviously taken aback, and he didn't hide his surprise as he shifted his weight and told her he already knew about "all that Jesus stuff." When my friend tried to ask some follow-up questions, he made sure the conversation ended quickly, and soon they went their separate ways (as much as two people can who are sharing the same eight square feet of space, that is).

Overhearing that conversation gave me a roller coaster of emotions that matched the condition of my stomach at high altitude. At first, I was cynical. *That all seemed forced.* Then I was embarrassed. *The entire encounter was uncomfortable.* Then I was discouraged. *She didn't get anywhere with him.* Then I was proud. *At least she went for it.* Then I was jealous. *I haven't said a word to anyone.* Then I was worried. *I'm a bad Christian.* Then I was cynical again. *This is stupid.*

I have been passionate about the gospel for many years now. It's the truth that changed my trajectory and continues to shape my life. The more I learn about myself, the more I realize my need for the gospel to infiltrate my thinking, overtake my rogue emotions, and transform my actions. But despite all that, I have spent most of my life not knowing how to proclaim the gospel to others. I have regularly felt a mixture of guilt (as I say nothing) and embarrassment (as I overhear others say awkward things).

To be honest, I think a bit of hesitancy is healthy when it comes to sharing the gospel. I don't think God intends for us to force or finagle our way into awkward conversations to try to convert people. My mistake was that I let that little bit of healthy hesitancy turn into a monster of insecurity, and for a while it kept me from obeying God's call on my life. But over the past several years, he has been opening my eyes and my heart to a new (more biblical) way of approaching evangelism, and it has liberated my day-to-day interactions with people.

When Kevin asked me to write this book with him, I got excited about the potential to bring people from a cynical, burned-out, and guilt-ridden relationship with evangelism to a place of freedom and fruitfulness. If you've spent your life as a Christian cringing at the thought of pulling out a napkin and drawing a chasm that only the Cross can span, you're in good company. For a long time I felt the same way. But don't let your cynicism, fear, or hesitancy keep you from joining God in what he is doing. There is a whole wide world of adventurous, fruitful, and authentic gospel-sharing that begins with the simple act of speaking up. My prayer is that this book will excite you and equip you for that.

Kevin and I find it a bit ironic that we are writing this book together. He was the kind of evangelist that made me cringe—and that I hoped to never be associated with. I was the kind of *non*-evangelist that Kevin judged and tried to compensate for. But that's why we believe this book will be relevant and helpful no matter which side of the spectrum you're starting from. This isn't a rejection of the gospel traditions we've come from; nor is it about finding the middle ground. Instead, it's an invitation for you to see how God has called us all to speak—by allowing our love for him to flow into our everyday language.

A SHEMA LIFESTYLE

Witnessing is not a spare-time occupation or a once-a-week activity. It must be a quality of life.

DAN GREENE

HAVE YOU EVER EXPERIENCED something like this? You move to a new town or a new neighborhood, and you're confident that God has put you there for a reason. Eager to reach your neighbors with the good news of Jesus, you're excited when the couple across the street seems interested in establishing a friendship. When they invite you over for dinner, you pray before you go, asking God to give you opportunities to engage them spiritually. You walk across the street full of hope and anticipation.

Over a delicious meal, you talk about your kids and your jobs and the weather—all the while wondering how you can bring up the subject of Jesus without it being awkward.

"Speaking of the weather, have you ever thought about whether you're going to heaven when you die?"

Nah, that's not the right approach. You don't want to be weird about it or force anything. You want the gospel to flow naturally into your conversations; and when it doesn't, you talk about other things instead. Afterward, you tell yourself it's not a big deal because you're in this for the long haul. You know there will be many more opportunities to share with your new friends. You'll say something next time.

But the next time comes and goes, and the time after that; before you know it, you've been living across the street from your friends for years and have never managed to find the "right time" to speak up about spiritual things. It's not for lack of desire. It's not for lack of prayer. You just don't know how to do it. You don't know where spiritual things fit into your everyday conversations, so you leave them out. And the longer it goes on this way, the more unlikely it is that you'll ever say anything about your faith in Jesus.

If this sounds familiar, don't think you're the only one with a story like this. Not by a long shot. The more I talk with people about evangelism, the more I realize that we *all* have our own version of "the failed attempt." Some have taken the route of silence. Others have tried their hand at steering the conversation. Some have never even gotten around to meeting their neighbors in the first place. But whatever the particular details might be, most Christians seem to struggle with how to share Jesus with the people around them.

In the church, the current prevailing concepts of evangelism have let us down. We've come to think of sharing the gospel as a *strategy* we employ rather than an *identity* we live out. Therefore, thinking strategically, we memorize a few facts about God's plan of salvation, devise some starter questions, and look for opportunities to insert them into conversations out of the blue. This approach tends to result in clumsy, irrelevant, and untimely ways of expressing our spirituality. It also leads to discouragement because many believers don't feel like themselves when using a scripted conversation. It doesn't fit who they are or how they think, and they start to wonder whether evangelism might be something better suited to a different type of person.

Before long, even the thought of evangelism carries with it feelings of anxiety, fear, apprehension, and guilt. Christians are tired of having awkward conversations that bear little to no fruit. And we're tired of interactions that don't reflect who we really are. Still, there's a constant tension building within us because we really want to be the kind of people who are brave and obedient and spread the gospel of Jesus. But we have no clue how to get from "How's the weather?" to "Jesus died for you."

The good news is that we feel the desire to share our faith. We feel the desire because we know that Jesus is the only path to life. We feel the desire because we know we are called to make disciples. And we feel the desire because we know that God is seeking and saving those who are lost, and we want to participate in what he is doing.

The bad news is that too many Christians have forgotten how to speak—or never learned how. They've kept their mouths shut about the gospel, even though it is the most compelling, transformative, life-giving message there is. The problem is that they don't know how to talk to people *simply* and *genuinely* about God.

How do you get into conversations that naturally lead to the gospel? How do you bring up the hope and promise of eternal life? This is where the bottleneck is, and it's why many believers rarely share about their faith.

But it doesn't have to be that way.

Maybe, like a lot of Christians, you are standing at the ready, equipped with the ability to give a compelling gospel presentation if the need should arise. And yet no one is walking up to you and asking, "What must I do to be saved?" If you find yourself waiting for opportunities that never seem to come, may we, in all humility, show you a more excellent way?

THE SHEMA

> Hear, O Israel: The LORD our God, the LORD is one. You
> shall love the LORD your God with all your heart and
> with all your soul and with all your might.
> DEUTERONOMY 6:4-5

Thousands of years ago, Moses delivered this command to the Israelites. Devout Jews ever since have started and ended each day by reciting it as a prayer that forms the beginning of a passage known as the Shema (Deuteronomy 6:4-9).[1] The words of the Shema were written on the doorways of Jewish homes, bound up in scrolls on their hands, and even placed on their foreheads. This passage had to be always within sight, always on their minds, and everywhere at the forefront of their actions.

The prayer begins with a word that means to *listen* or *hear*: "Hear, O Israel . . ." But this word, *shema*, doesn't align with the simple English definition of "hearing." In English, we can "hear" something but disregard it. That's why frustrated parents sometimes yell at their kids, "Are you even listening to me?" We often think of hearing as simply knowing that someone is talking to us, and it can be disconnected from responding to what the person says.

But in Hebrew, *shema* is altogether different. It means to *listen attentively* and *respond obediently*. Shema is the act of giving our attention to something so fully that hearing and doing become one and the same. Proclaiming that "the LORD our God . . . is one" becomes "loving him with all our heart and soul and might." In other words, our response to God's character is to love him with all that we are.

Though the Shema has been foundational to Judaism since the time of Moses, it is not confined to Jewish tradition. Jesus said that the Shema is the pinnacle of the Christian walk as well. To "love the Lord . . . with all your heart . . . soul . . . mind and . . . strength" is the commandment to sum up all commandments.[2] In other words, the Shema is an incredibly important concept for anyone who is interested in following Jesus.

When Moses gave the Shema, he didn't just tell the people *what* to do; he also told them *how* to do it:

> These words that I command you today shall be on your
> heart. You shall teach them diligently to your children,
> and shall talk of them when you sit in your house, and
> when you walk by the way, and when you lie down, and
> when you rise.
> DEUTERONOMY 6:6-7

The most tangible expression of your love for God is talking about him. When you get up in the morning, talk about God. When you're walking down the street, talk about God.

When you are sitting at home, taking your kids to the park, eating at a restaurant, or commuting to work, talk about God. God should be at the forefront of your mind. You should speak like a person who is almost preoccupied with him. Everything points to him, relates to him, comes from him, reflects him, reminds you of him—and you can't help but express it in almost everything you say. The more deeply and fully you love God, the more naturally this language will flow out of you.

When I say that we should talk about God, I don't mean simply dropping Christian jargon into our daily conversations. Rather, as part of our vernacular, we should make statements that point to spiritual realities and the presence of God in our lives. We should say the spiritual things that come to our minds as we talk with others. This doesn't necessarily mean sharing the gospel with everyone we meet. It just means using simple statements to show that we are followers of God. In chapter 6, we will talk more specifically about what those simple statements can look like.

Moses further instructed the Israelites:

You shall bind [these words] as a sign on your hand, and they shall be as frontlets between your eyes. You shall write them on the doorposts of your house and on your gates.
DEUTERONOMY 6:8-9

Some Jewish people have taken these verses very literally throughout history. In New York City today, you will sometimes see Hassidic Jews with small leather boxes attached to their heads. These boxes are called phylacteries, and they contain the words of the Shema. Phylacteries are frontlets between their eyes. It's the first thing you notice about them. You can't pretend it isn't there. It's obvious that they are Jewish because they are literally wearing a sign across their foreheads.

Even if we don't practice the commands literally, there is deep meaning in these verses for us as followers of Jesus—both in our private walk with God and in the way we make our faith known to others.

When we bind God's truths on our hands or write them on our doorposts, they are something only we will see. They serve as a personal reminder of what our lives should be devoted to. When we strap them across our foreheads or write them on our front gates, they act as a sign to everyone. They become an obvious proclamation of what our lives are devoted to. In giving us the Shema, Moses was pointing to the fact that God is at the center of *everything* we say and do—both public and private.

As Christians, we don't wear phylacteries or place mezuzahs (small parchment scrolls, containing the words of the Shema, in decorative cases) on our doorposts, but we can and should follow the Shema in how we speak—both inside and outside our homes. From the moment we enter a conversation with others, they will be able to tell that we are spiritual because it will be obvious in our language—so obvious that we might as well be wearing a sign on our foreheads. This is one example of how we love God with everything we are. We become so enamored of him that we can't help but talk about him in obvious ways, in every context.

If you have the desire to share the gospel but feel burned out, afraid, or awkward; if you tend to remain silent because you don't know how to bring it up; or if you haven't figured out where God fits into your conversations, so you leave him out altogether—I have some good news for you. Moses gave us the answer thousands of years ago, and Jesus reiterated it: God fits *everywhere*, into *every* conversation. When we know him, we love him; when we love him, we can't help but talk about him.

These verses in Deuteronomy, and their corresponding passages in the Gospels, have incredible implications for evangelism. If sharing our love for God is less about memorizing the right words and more about letting the natural words flow out of us, then the bottleneck disappears. We don't have to worry about how to bring up the gospel because the Shema is not a strategy for sharing the gospel; it's a way of living that begets the gospel. Spiritual people talking about spiritual things naturally leads to spiritual engagement.

This is what I like to call *living out loud*:

- *Living*: It's an active, natural posture of loving God and talking about him as we go about our daily lives.
- *Out*: Our love for God spills over into everything we say and do.
- *Loud*: This doesn't mean we turn up the volume to draw attention to ourselves, but rather that we talk about God in ways that are *obvious* to the people around us. Think *loud and clear*.

Living out loud doesn't mean we're flamboyant, obnoxious, or provocative. It simply means that we bring the same enthusiasm to talking about God that we naturally demonstrate when talking about other things we're excited about and committed to and that we believe are important.

DELIVERY GUY

I have been on a journey of living out loud for many years. I am nowhere near perfect at it, but what I can tell you is that it gets easier and becomes more and more natural to talk about God in every situation. Along with that, it becomes more likely that we will see fruit in the most *un*likely places.

When I began to let my love for God flow into my everyday language, even something as ordinary as ordering pizza became an opportunity to see God move. And a simple spiritual statement changed the course of a conversation—and, ultimately, the course of a friendship.

One Monday night, there was a knock at my door. This was not unexpected, because I had ordered a pizza earlier. As the delivery guy handed me the warm boxes, I asked him his name.

"Muhammad," he said.

We got to talking a bit, and Muhammad told me he was from Senegal.

"That's really cool," I said, "because God is doing amazing things among your people."

"What do you mean?" he asked.

I told him that God was speaking to people in dreams and visions, and people were coming to know Jesus.

Muhammad and I became friends that day. We exchanged phone numbers and started meeting twice a week. My house was on the way to the pizza place where he worked, and we would often get together to talk and pray before he started his shifts.

Eventually Muhammad moved back to Senegal. But before he did, he had read Scriptures with me and heard me talk about Jesus; he knew how to pray to him and had learned a bit about trusting him.

That Monday night when I ordered the pizza, I had no evangelistic strategy in mind. I wasn't trying to lure someone to my door so I could hit them with the gospel message. I ordered the pizza because I was hungry. When Muhammad brought it to my door, I didn't have a plan to engage him spiritually. Our conversation went where it did because I didn't bite my tongue when a spiritual thought came to mind. And because, as it turned out, Muhammad was hungry too.

Our misguided ideas about evangelism have left us jaded and kept us silent. But I believe there's a better way. In the pages that follow, we will show you that there is a biblical case for why spiritual engagement includes simply speaking up. We can't err on the side of saying nothing and hope that our actions alone will bring people to Jesus. We must open our mouths. We will show you that engaging people spiritually can be a regular, natural, genuine rhythm of life for every follower of Jesus. Yes, including you. It won't require you to check your personality at the door or use techniques that don't fit who you are or the situations you're in.

As you discover these truths, our goal is to give you a new vision for spiritual engagement—one that will help you move away from feelings of fear and awkwardness and toward the freedom of letting your love for God spill into your everyday language.

A NEW TYPE OF PERSON

God became man to turn creatures into sons: not simply to
produce better men of the old kind but to produce a new
kind of man. It is not like teaching a horse to jump better
and better but like turning a horse into a winged creature.

C. S. LEWIS

I GREW UP IN A ROW HOUSE in Philadelphia. My neighborhood was devoid of grass, and nature was more of a concept than
a reality for me. All that to say, I'm not much of a camper. I like it,
but I would probably die if I became stranded in the wild. This is
most evident in my inability to start a fire. A good outdoorsman
can rub two sticks together and create a spark. I cannot. There is
a special technique, and only once you've mastered that technique
are you able to see a fire ignite.

This is how many Christians think about evangelism: "If I
could just learn the right technique, I would be successful." But as
followers of Jesus, we are new creations. And when we were made
new, a fire not of our own making was ignited inside us. Unlike
starting a campfire, evangelism doesn't require us to spark a flame.

The Holy Spirit is the Great Initiator; we just need to let him do his thing.

It comes down to understanding who we are.

In 2 Corinthians 5:17, Paul says that anyone who is in Christ "is a new creation. The old has passed away." In Ephesians, Paul tells us, "Put off your old self, which belongs to your former manner of life . . . be renewed in the spirit of your minds, and . . . put on the new self, created after the likeness of God in true righteousness and holiness."[1] Both of these passages highlight the reality that, through Jesus, who we are—our very nature, likeness, and self—is made different, entirely new, and unlike what we were before.

Do you believe it?

Maybe as you're reading this you're thinking about all the ways in which you seem like the same old person. But notice that Paul doesn't say, "If you *feel* like a new creation, then you are a new creation." He doesn't say, "If you start *acting* like a new creation, then you are a new creation." No, the truth is that, if you are in Christ, the substance of who you are has changed. Believing this reality—and living into this reality—is one of the most faith-filled things we can do. And that's when evangelism really comes alive.

If the substance of who we are has changed, what has it changed into? Who are we as new creations? The Bible offers three compelling metaphors to describe our new selves, and each one has ramifications for spiritual engagement.

WE ARE SALT

In the Sermon on the Mount, Jesus calls his followers "the salt of the earth."[2] That is to say, we are the kind of presence in the world that changes it. The late British theologian John Stott put it like this: "God intends us to penetrate the world. Christian salt has no business to remain snugly in elegant little ecclesiastical salt cellars; our place is to be rubbed into the secular community, as salt is rubbed into meat, to stop it going bad."[3]

By its very nature, salt is effective. If you've ever walked near the ocean, you may have noticed a tinge in the air, felt the grit on your skin, and seen the erosion on piers and bridges. Salt changes the landscape just by being present in the water and air. It changes the chemistry of food when added as an ingredient. As Christians, we are spiritual salt in the world, and our very presence changes things.

WE ARE AN AROMA

We are the aroma of Christ to God among those who are being saved and among those who are perishing, to one a fragrance from death to death, to the other a fragrance from life to life.

2 CORINTHIANS 2:15-16

In the Roman Empire, a returning conqueror would fill the air with perfume as he arrived home, declaring his victory. People would line the streets and take in the aroma of the general's triumph. For some, it would be a smell that evoked celebration, but for those who were conquered, it was the smell of defeat.[4] This is the idea Paul is drawing upon in 2 Corinthians. We are the aroma that announces Christ the Conqueror.

As a native Philadelphian, I often went to Hershey, PA, home of the old Hershey's Chocolate factory. The factory was so successful that they also opened a theme park called Hersheypark. Back in the day, when the original factory was operating (which was pretty much all the time), the aroma of chocolate permeated the entire town.

That's what a powerful fragrance does—it makes an impact on the environment around it. "We are the aroma of Christ" in this world.[5] Our spiritual presence is pervasive.

WE ARE LIGHT

Also in the Sermon on the Mount, Jesus calls his followers "the light of the world."[6] Our new nature is such that it "cannot be hidden" but "gives light to all in the house."[7] The reason a lighthouse exists is to keep ships safe from wrecking. Its beacon shines into the dark of the night, warning seafarers of the impending shore. Its light pierces through raging storms, helping orient those at the helm. It is trustworthy and steadfast because light always overcomes darkness. Light cannot be overlooked because, by its very nature, it transforms the space around it. So it is with us and our new nature. Like a city on a hill or a lamp on a stand, our new nature defeats the darkness, acts like a beacon, and reveals what is hidden.

Though each of these metaphors defines a different aspect of Christian character, they all demonstrate at least one common truth: The very essence of our new nature has an impact on the people around us. Our presence in the world isn't wishy-washy or indistinct; it is potent. Just as salt affects the flavor and nature of food, just as an aroma fills a space and floods our senses, and just as light overwhelms the shadows, our new nature flavors and fills and floods and overwhelms the environment around us. When we step onto an elevator, join a line, or sit in a booth, we radiate a new quality of being—the kind that changes the atmosphere.

HEAR THE LIGHT

The metaphor of light is particularly interesting to me because we can miss the scope of what it means for us. If, in our new nature, we are a powerful and pervasive light that invades everywhere we go, how is it that we manage to have so many mundane interactions? How come no one accepted Jesus last time we went grocery shopping? Why is no one using words such as *bright* or *glimmering* to describe us? As I asked these questions of myself, I realized I had been missing the primary way we are called to function as light.

I was familiar with the biblical concept of letting my light shine, and I knew it had something to do with my actions. I figured the best way to be a light in my community was to be kind and generous and patient, and eventually my neighbors would recognize these traits in me and ask me about Jesus. But as I read Scripture, I began to realize that being a light is about more than just my actions. If I was going to be an illuminating presence drawing people to Jesus, my presence had to include *words*. My light would shine through the words of my mouth.

Isn't it just like God to take something and turn it on its head—to take light and make it something that people need to *hear*?

> I have come into the world as light, so that whoever believes in me may not remain in darkness. If anyone hears my words and does not keep them, I do not judge him; for I did not come to judge the world but to save the world.
> JOHN 12:46-47

Here Jesus says that he came into the world as a light, able to draw people out of darkness through the hearing of his words. His ministry was one of light and one of words. If people were going to recognize Jesus as light, they needed to hear what he said.

> There is another who bears witness about me, and I know that the testimony that he bears about me is true. You sent to John, and he has borne witness to the truth. Not that the testimony that I receive is from man, but I say these things so that you may be saved. He was a burning and shining lamp, and you were willing to rejoice for a while in his light.
>
> JOHN 5:32-35

This passage is about John the Baptist—what he did and who he was. He did the work of an evangelist, bearing witness to the truth of Jesus through speaking.

He was a burning and shining lamp whose light caused others to rejoice. In other words, John *spoke* about Jesus, and by speaking, he functioned as a light.

We also see this with Paul and Barnabas:

> Paul and Barnabas spoke out boldly, saying, "It was necessary that the word of God be spoken first to you. Since you thrust it aside and judge yourselves unworthy of eternal life, behold, we are turning to the Gentiles. For so the Lord has commanded us, saying,
>
> "'I have made you a light for the Gentiles,
>   that you may bring salvation to the ends of the earth.'"

And when the Gentiles heard this, they began rejoicing and glorifying the word of the Lord, and as many as were appointed to eternal life believed. And the word of the Lord was spreading throughout the whole region.

ACTS 13:46-49

Paul and Barnabas describe their ministry as a calling from God to be "a light for the Gentiles." They fulfilled this calling by speaking the word of God. They operated as lights, the word of God spread, and many believed through hearing. So again, light is linked to speech.

Each of these passages seems to point to the fact that being light in the world is about more than just trying to be neighborly. I used to think that I needed to talk differently around unbelievers. I would carefully navigate conversations, leaving out tidbits of spiritual thoughts and biblical perspectives, and then feel lost as to how to get the conversation around to the gospel. Ironically, I felt as if the right way to engage people spiritually was to begin by suppressing my spirituality. I didn't realize that, as a new creation, I am designed to be a potently contrasting presence. I was trying to preach the gospel in a dark world without shining my light.

SUBWAY RIDES

Wendy belongs to our house church network. She is the kind of person who operates as a new creation in Christ. As she commutes to work on the subway each morning, she prays for God to use her and to make her the kind of presence that draws people to himself.

I like to picture the dreary atmosphere on that dark subway. There's a sort of lull that falls over a bunch of tired people on their way to work. And then I think about Wendy stepping onto the train. No one can see it at first, but maybe some can sense it: A light has appeared in the midst of the fog. There's a tinge of saltiness in the air and an aroma of grace wafting over the seats.

Because Wendy is filled with the Holy Spirit and she knows the kind of hope she has within her, she anticipates that her subway rides will turn into sacred encounters. And quite often they do. Just the other day, she was praying as she stepped into the subway car, asking, "Lord, guide me to the person you want me to sit next to." Then she sat where she felt God was leading her.

She smiled politely at the woman next to her and quietly pulled out her Bible (which is also part of her daily routine). As Wendy was reading, the woman leaned over and asked her about it. Wendy shared what she was reading, and that launched a conversation about God. The woman told Wendy that she had been searching, and Wendy told her about how God had changed her life. There was nothing contrived or forced about the conversation. It was simply two women on their way to work, sharing their lives together for a few minutes. But what set this conversation apart from the thousands of others on the subway that day was that Wendy wasn't afraid to talk about what God had done in her life. In fact, she was ready, willing, and able.

It's exciting to think of the impact we can have simply by being who we are, wherever we are. Wendy didn't stand on the subway platform and preach a well-crafted sermon. She commuted to work in the knowledge that she is a potent presence, and she allowed God to use her however he saw fit.

Because of her love for God, Wendy is a light in her world. And because she opened her mouth to let that love spill out, her light did what it was designed to do.

You've no doubt heard the admonition, often attributed to Francis of Assisi, "Preach the gospel at all times. Use words if necessary."[8] There's no evidence that Francis ever said that, and in any case I think Scripture points to a deeper call on our lives, one that is both exciting and possibly a bit intimidating: We should preach the gospel at all times, and whenever *possible*, use words. Whenever we have an opportunity to be ourselves and express our love for God, whenever we hope to draw people toward him, whenever we desire to make an atmospheric impact, we should be ready to open our mouths as people who have been radically transformed into something new. As Duane Litfin, former president of Wheaton College, says, "It's simply not possible to preach the gospel without words. The gospel is inherently a *verbal* thing, and preaching the gospel is inherently a *verbal* behavior."[9]

Understanding ourselves as new creations is the beginning of living out loud. If you and I catch the biblical vision of our newness in Christ, we can start to engage people spiritually because we think and speak and act as spiritual beings. If we catch the vision of our potency as new creations, we can enter conversations with the confidence that we are intended to shift conversational tides. If we catch the vision of ourselves as light, we can recognize the importance of our words and allow our speech to be saturated with our love for God.

Catching the vision of who we are in Christ changes everything about how we approach evangelism. Namely, we don't "approach" it at all. We *live* it. Sharing the gospel is a natural byproduct of being who we are. Like salt, we are transformative. Like a fragrant aroma, we are potent. Like light, we are visible, not hidden. We are spiritually new, altogether different, and we cause a marked change in the atmosphere of daily life simply by being ourselves and living out loud.

TODAY'S HARVEST

More winnable people live in the world today than ever
before, . . . [But] if, in the day of harvest, . . . [God's] servants
fail him, then the ripened grain will not be harvested.
DONALD A. MCGAVRAN

OUR WILLINGNESS TO ENGAGE people spiritually depends not
only on *who* we are but *where* we are. Landscape matters. You and
I would approach walking through a jungle very differently than
we would strolling through a park. We alter our behavior based
on our surroundings.

According to a 2018 study by Barna, 48 percent of Christians
in the US believe the people around them "have no interest in
hearing about Jesus" (up from 45 percent in 1993). Another
28 percent say they are "unsure" whether non-Christians would
be interested in hearing about Jesus (up from 5 percent in 1993).[1]
These statistics are probably not all that surprising. Many of us
operate with an underlying assumption that our attempts to
engage people spiritually will fall short. It seems like common

sense, doesn't it? We expect to be rejected because we assume we will talk to one hundred unreceptive people for every one person who wants to listen. But the Bible paints a very different picture of the landscape.

In Luke 10, Jesus sends seventy-two of his followers out into the neighboring towns he will soon visit. He knows they will face hardship. He knows that, at times, they will be rejected. But they will also find people of peace. They are to eat and to stay with such people and to preach the gospel wherever they are made welcome.

As Jesus prepares them to go, he encourages them with one important detail about the terrain. In fact, it is so important that it will affect everything about how they go out into the world. And because that one important fact hasn't changed in more than two thousand years, what Jesus said will affect everything about how you and I go out into the world. It will affect our expectations of *what* God will do, *how* he will use us, *who* we decide to engage, *why* we strike up conversations, *when* we speak about spiritual things, and *where* we look for God to move.

So what did Jesus tell his disciples that was so important it changed everything? Simply this: "The harvest is plentiful."[2]

The seventy-two needed to understand the nature of their surroundings. Jesus wasn't talking about wheat, of course. He was talking about people. He wanted his disciples to see past the obvious distinctions between Jew, Gentile, mother, father, stranger, and friend, and catch a glimpse of the greater reality behind the obvious. He wanted them to see the thousands of hearts God was *already* stirring. He wanted them to know that every assumption and apprehension was only background noise when God was moving and hearts were ripening.

In John 4:35, Jesus says, "Look, I tell you, lift up your eyes, and see that the fields are white for harvest." In other words, look around at your workplace, your neighborhood, the grocery store, the shopping mall, the airport, or the subway station, and have the sort of eyes that see throngs of people ready to hear the gospel—so ready that they are like heads of wheat bursting at the seams.

God is always at work,[3] and he is "making his appeal through us."[4] We are not only living in the midst of harvestable fields, but we also have a God who is actively working in those fields. Right now, *today*, people are being drawn toward him. People are hearing his voice and responding. God is making his appeal, he is using us to do it, and people are ready to listen. That is the reality of our landscape—many eager people; many stirring hearts; many longing for hope, waiting to hear and ready to receive the Good News.

What does this mean practically? It means that wherever you are right now, there are hundreds, maybe thousands, of people all around you who are spiritually open and ready to be receptive to Christ. These people are in the office, at the park, on the bus, in restaurants and cafes, in synagogues and mosques. And they are ready to hear from God!

If we truly believed we were in the midst of a plentiful harvest, it would change everything about how we go out into the world. If we were convinced that thousands of people around us were ready to put their trust in Jesus, it would change our posture in how we engage them. So why don't we? Why do we act as if we believe God is stagnant and people are too far gone? Why do we assume God has stopped working the way he once did?

We see a crowd of people just waiting to take offense. Jesus says there is actually an abundant harvest waiting for us to speak up. We look at our neighbors and coworkers and assume they are uninterested. Jesus says, "Open your eyes and look at the fields! They are ripe for harvest."[5] We anticipate rejection. Jesus is seeking and saving the lost.[6] Why do we have such a hard time seeing it?

SEEING IS BELIEVING

The Bible teaches that there are realities we can't see. There is a spiritual realm that exists beyond this world, and only the eyes of faith have a chance of catching a glimpse this side of heaven.[7] Faith illuminates, reveals, and offers a window into the fullest picture of reality. When two people have different degrees of faith, they will walk through the same experience hearing and seeing it very differently.

This reminds me of the prophet Elisha and his servant in 2 Kings 6. There was a raiding nation at war with Israel, and fear permeated the hearts of the people. But Elisha knew something the others didn't. He could see something they couldn't. When the opposing king sent his army to surround the city, Elisha's servant cried out in fear. But Elisha prayed that God would give the young man eyes to see. All of a sudden, as the servant looked at the hills, he saw another army surrounding the city—one made of fire from God. Before his eyes were opened, Elisha's servant was seeing reality, but he was only seeing it in part. He and Elisha were facing the same battle, looking at the same situation, but experiencing two very different realities. Only when his eyes were opened to the complete landscape did the servant realize the scope of what God was doing and that everything was well in hand.

The same is true for us. It's interesting how two people can live in the same city, be part of the same church, maybe even live on the same street, and yet experience two very different realities of spiritual awareness and fruitfulness. How is this possible? The answer lies in what they believe. It's all a matter of faith.

Faith gives us eyes to see the true desperateness of the lost, the true readiness of the harvest, and the countless opportunities for spiritual engagement. Jesus cast a vision for a plentiful harvest; faith enables our eyes to behold it.

How is it that the water can be empty and silent, and yet when Jesus says, "Cast the net on the right side of the boat,"[8] the catch turns out to be massive? The disciples were professional fishermen, using every skill they had to look for fish, but they found nothing until Jesus came. They were in an environment devoid of fish until Jesus invaded the landscape. I have often wondered whether Jesus changed the condition of the water or just the vision of the fishermen. Were the fish there, and the men couldn't see them below the reach of their nets? Or did Jesus make them appear? Whether it was a miracle or just a glimpse into a deeper reality, it characterizes the experience of those who walk by faith.

What does it mean to walk by faith? The mental, spiritual, and possibly even physical experience of faith is the feeling or sense of expectation. You believe something will happen, and you are eagerly waiting for it. It's like getting ready to swing the bat as the pitcher winds up. Living with this kind of anticipation will make all the difference in how we engage people. We will either meet them with expectancy or pass by them without ever seeing what God might do.

Imagine what it would feel like to walk out your front door every morning utterly convinced that you will encounter people whom God is drawing to himself. How would your interactions with people change if you firmly believed that God was making his appeal through *you*? What if you saw your daily routine as a walk through a multitude of harvestable crops? How would you engage people differently if you believed every conversation was an opportunity to check for ripeness?

Faith, it has been said, is the currency of heaven. Everything we experience and have in the spiritual realm is bought by faith. Everything we get to see in the Kingdom of God is seen through eyes of faith. Any power that flows through us, in the display of God's glory, is by faith. Without faith it is impossible to please God.[9]

Without faith, the fields are dry and barren. But *with* faith, the harvest is plentiful. With faith, there are crops ripe for the picking. There are receptive hearts and opportunities waiting. There are armies of fire and bursting nets—and it's happening all around us if only we could see. If we could walk down the sidewalk and assume that God is moving in our midst, we just might come to find that every interaction is of eternal consequence.

We alter our behavior based on our terrain, and the truth is that you and I are standing in the midst of some very harvestable fields. Our willingness to engage people spiritually will depend on our willingness and our ability to embrace this reality. We will either enter conversations with anticipatory faith, or we won't. The biblical picture of a plentiful harvest sweeps away our apprehensive and guilt-ridden ideas about evangelism and opens our eyes to a world waiting to be engaged and won for Christ. That reality becomes an invitation for us to live out loud and to see autumn-like dividends as God seeks and saves those around us.

PRODIGAL FARMING

How you believe God perceives people
will determine how you respond to them.
JACQUELYN K. HEASLEY

IN 1906, NAVAL ARCHITECT LEWIS NIXON invented an
underwater listening device to help ships navigate around icebergs.[1] Sadly, this device was not in use six years later when the
Titanic, considered to be an unsinkable ship, hit an iceberg and
sank, killing 1,500 people. With later contributions from scien-
tists such as Reginald Fessenden, Paul Langevin, and Constantin
Chilowski, the technology evolved into what we now know as
sonar, which remains the most common way to detect underwater
objects.[2]

What does sonar have to do with living out loud? A lot more
than you may think. Maybe you struggle to believe that the harvest is plentiful, because your personal track record indicates the
opposite. Maybe you've looked and looked for opportunities to
engage people spiritually but to no avail. You can't seem to find

the people who are supposedly ripe for the harvest. From where you stand, things seem a whole lot more like a wasteland than a flourishing field.

If this describes how you feel, you may be approaching spiritual engagement like a sonar operator. Perhaps you've come to believe (even if subconsciously) that you need to develop some sort of special ability that will allow you to detect the people who are spiritually receptive. Maybe you think of engaging people as a two-step process:

Step 1. Develop a special "sonar" that can detect spiritually receptive people.
Step 2. Engage those people with spiritual things.

This approach has some problems. First, we usually aren't very good at gauging spiritual receptivity. Instead, we jump to conclusions about people. If someone looks rich or important, we assume they won't be spiritually receptive. If someone adheres to a different religion, we assume they won't be interested in the gospel. But we really can't trust our ability to gauge spiritual receptivity, because we tend to look at the wrong things.

One classic misconception is that we can measure a person's level of interest in Jesus based on their level of interest in attending a church service. But that's not a good barometer for spiritual engagement. Church services aren't the Good News; Jesus is. Inviting people to attend a church gathering is not the same thing as sharing the gospel with them, and their response to our invitation to church is not a good indication of their spiritual receptivity. Sometimes the same people who are least likely to set foot inside a church building are the very people most likely to respond to the gospel.

When *The Passion of the Christ* was released in 2004, movie theaters were sold out across the country. In the newspaper one day, I saw a cartoon of a church building next to a movie theater. In front of the church stood an elderly couple clenching their Bibles and looking rather lonely. Meanwhile, the theater next door had a line of people stretching around the block, all waiting to see this new movie about Jesus. The point of the cartoon was clear: Just because people aren't interested in church doesn't mean they aren't interested in Jesus.

Another problem with the sonar approach is that it really isn't our job to walk around determining who will and won't be receptive. In fact, it's incredibly arrogant to think we could take on that role. I've known many Christians who didn't give off "spiritually receptive" vibes before they became believers. Every conversion is a miraculous act of God. Spiritual receptivity isn't something we can detect from far away. Besides, when we try to use receptivity as the basis of our interactions with people, we've gotten the order all wrong. Spiritual receptivity is something we discover *as* we engage with people, not *before* we engage with them. The better way to interact with others is like this:

Step 1. Engage people with spiritual things.
Step 2. Through engaging, find those who are spiritually receptive.

If finding spiritually receptive people is like looking for a needle in a haystack, then, yeah, let's methodically sift through all the hay until we find that one shiny needle. But if Jesus is right (which he is) and the harvest is plentiful (which it is), then we need an approach that doesn't rely on our ability to differentiate between needles and hay. Rather than acting like sonar operators, who are specially trained to operate complicated equipment and detect the presence of icebergs or other ships, our job is closer to that of an irresponsible farmer who casts seed everywhere without discretion.

> A sower went out to sow. And as he sowed, some seeds fell along the path, and the birds came and devoured them. Other seeds fell on rocky ground, where they did not have much soil, and immediately they sprang up, since they had no depth of soil, but when the sun rose, they were scorched. And since they had no root, they withered away. Other seeds fell among thorns, and the thorns grew up and choked them. Other seeds fell on good soil and produced grain, some a hundredfold, some sixty, some thirty.
>
> MATTHEW 13:3-8

Modern farming is not haphazard. It's methodical. Rows are tilled into fertilized soil. Seed is meticulously planted in each row. Crop yields are calculated, planned, arranged. But not in Jesus' parable. Instead, he paints a picture of a farmer who seems almost careless with his seed. He walks through his fields, casting it every which way, letting it land wherever it will—and some of it takes root.

The lesson often taught from this parable is that the gospel will reach people differently, and people will respond to it differently. For some it will grow into something; for others it won't. But a secondary lesson we can learn from this parable is the method by which the gospel goes out—abundantly, overwhelmingly, almost flippantly, reaching all kinds of people in all different stages of receptivity. The more seed that gets scattered, the greater the chance it will land somewhere good.

As we look more closely at the haphazard farmer, we find four key principles for how to engage people with spiritual things:

1. Scatter the seed generously because we don't know where the best soil is

We run a program in New York City called Seed Weeks, which is designed to train people in cross-cultural ministry and give them tools to engage people spiritually. After prayer and training each day, participants go out on the streets to talk with people. Every year, I see the same thing: The groups all gravitate toward the homeless population.

Why? Because a homeless person with a ton of need and nowhere to go seems like an easier person to share the gospel with than a businessperson, who seems more important than us. Fear, skepticism, and ease of connection are not the criteria we are called to use in deciding who to engage. Businesspeople are not necessarily rocky soil, and homeless people are not necessarily good soil. We are called to cast seed as if we have no clue where the most abundant harvest will come from—because we don't. Regardless, the method remains the same: indiscriminate seed throwing—that is, to everyone, everywhere.

2. Scatter the seed generously because that is how to reap abundantly

The more seed we throw, the greater the harvest will be. I have seen it time and again: The people who sow the most reap the most. Yes, it's true that there will be times when nothing sprouts at all. There will be times when it seems like the seed is going to take hold, then doesn't last. But eventually, and inevitably, there will be times when the seed puts down deep roots and grows into something good.

Farmers don't expect to find a harvest where no seed has been planted. They know if they want a big harvest, they must scatter a lot of seed. Likewise with sharing the gospel. The more people we engage, the more people we reach. Because we've been promised an abundant harvest, we are called to cast seed *as if* it will take root and grow. The result of our believing this promise should be abundant, generous, unstinting, even prodigal seed throwing.

3. Scatter the seed generously because we have plenty

Farmers typically conserve their seed. Seed is a precious commodity and shouldn't be wasted. That's why it's reserved for soil that has been tested and proven to be rich and viable. But the farmer in the parable has no notion of hoarding his seed. He casts it without concern for running out.

The same is true for us with our spiritual engagement. There's no need to be stingy. We don't run the risk of depletion. We don't need to worry about engaging too many people or saying too many authentically spiritual things or wasting words on "bad soil." We don't have to hold back, testing spiritual conditions for viability before we say something. We are spiritual people who will never run out of opportunities. The byproduct of this should be lavish, constant, perpetual seed throwing.

4. Scatter the seed generously because that is our calling

Farmers cast seed; it's what they do. Spiritual people engage people spiritually; it's what we do. The natural overflow of our being a new creation is that we walk around having spiritual thoughts, saying spiritual things, and making a spiritual impact. Our new life in Christ is not something we turn on and off as a strategy for gospel sharing. It is *who we are*. We need to learn how to be comfortable in our own (new) skin. We are called to cast seed as a way of life. The natural result should be extravagant, unaffected, sincere, and authentic seed throwing.

LIVING OUT LOUD AS PRODIGAL FARMERS

When I spoke recently at a church about the idea of living out loud, I explained how it was easy, through common statements, to let people know we are spiritual people. I also said that when we live authentically as spiritual people, we will find people all around us who are spiritually receptive. Later that day, as I was still driving back home to New York, the pastor of the church called me.

"Kev, guess what just happened?" he said. "After your talk today, a guy from my church was inspired to turn up his spiritual volume. Right after the service, he went home and saw his next-door neighbor out in the yard, picking up sticks. So he went over to talk to him. They've been next-door neighbors for ten years but have never talked about spiritual things. I guess my guy thought his neighbor wouldn't be interested—or at least *feared* he wouldn't.

"As they talked about normal, surface sorts of things, the guy from my church was wondering how to apply what you said and be openly spiritual. So he asked his neighbor, 'Joe, is there anything I can pray for you about?' Immediately the man's eyes filled with tears. He shared about how his marriage is falling apart and his daughter won't speak to him. Before my guy knew it, he was praying for his neighbor as the man sobbed out in the yard. For ten years he had said nothing. But it sounds like all he needed to do was ask his neighbor if he could pray for him, and the guy's heart cracked wide open. My guy said he couldn't believe how long it has taken him to open his mouth. Kevin, he was so shocked at how God worked that he called me right away and told me the story. I just wanted you to know that your words struck home."

When we try to detect spiritual receptivity and make it a prerequisite for our willingness to engage someone, we will never engage with anyone. We will be stingy farmers—hoarding our seed as we try to determine what type of soil is underneath the surface of someone's demeanor. But the truth is, we never really know what's going on inside other people or what might grow into something good. As cross-cultural church planter Elliot Clark writes, "If we continue the pattern of waiting for perfect opportunities, they may never come. And our fate will be that of the wary farmer who observes the wind and doesn't sow, who considers the clouds and never reaps (Ecclesiastes 11:4). Such farmers have empty barns in winter."[3]

We are new creations whose very essence has been transformed into a potent, influential substance; and we find ourselves in a world packed with people whom God is drawing to himself. Our workplaces and our gyms, our neighborhoods, and even our own yards are brimming with opportunities. We might as well walk around striking up conversations and casting seed every which way, because when we speak as spiritual people, we will start to find people who are receptive to spiritual things. No sonar needed.

THE SPIRIT MOVES MOUTHS

*I don't want my life to be explainable
without the Holy Spirit.*

FRANCIS CHAN

THE BOOK OF ACTS is a narrative that winds through the lives of Jesus' followers. It tells us what the early church did in the wake of Christ's ascension. God wanted us to have a vivid account of what it looked like when people who walked with Jesus were given the Holy Spirit and were called into a new kind of living. Acts shows us how Christianity became the seedbed of radical community, ambitious evangelism, humble love, sacrificial generosity, and supernatural transformation.

During those early days, the Holy Spirit was healing, guiding, and saving people around every corner. But the Spirit was also working in a more subtle way. We can almost miss it if we aren't paying attention. Acts shows us that when the Holy Spirit, God's Helper (sent to empower his people) shows up, people *speak.*

Over and over again, people encounter the Spirit and respond verbally—prophesying, proclaiming, speaking, asking, witnessing, testifying—with a profusion of Spirit-inspired words.

- In Acts 1:8, Jesus says that, as a result of the Holy Spirit coming upon the church, they would become *witnesses*.
- Acts 2:4 shows how believers were filled with the Spirit and began *speaking* in other tongues.
- Acts 2:17-18 says that people would *prophesy* when Jesus poured out his Spirit.
- In Acts 4:8, Peter *speaks* to people as a result of being filled with the Spirit.
- In Acts 4:31, believers were suddenly filled with the Spirit and began *speaking* the word of God *boldly*.
- In Acts 6:10, some community leaders were trying to dispute Stephen, but they couldn't because he was *speaking in the Spirit*.
- Acts 7:55-56 shows the Spirit giving Stephen a supernatural glimpse into heaven, and Stephen's response is to *talk* about it.
- In Acts 8:29-30, Philip is led by the Spirit to go to the Ethiopian man in order to *talk* to him about the Scriptures.
- Acts 11:12-15 is Peter's retelling of a time when the Spirit moved him to step outside his comfort zone, go to the home of a Roman military officer, and *speak* to the people there.
- In Acts 11:28, Agabus *foretells* through the Spirit that there will be a famine.
- In Acts 13:9-10, Paul is filled with the Spirit and then turns and *speaks* to Elymas.
- Acts 19:6 talks about people beginning to *speak in tongues* and *prophesy* after the coming of the Holy Spirit upon them.

Before his ascension, Jesus promised to send us the Holy Spirit as a divine helper. He said that having the Spirit would be even better than if Jesus himself were to stay. The Holy Spirit isn't a second-rate consolation prize. The Spirit is the very essence and power of God working in and through us. When the Holy Spirit empowers people, they are capable of extraordinary things. One primary way the Spirit's power manifests itself in our lives is by emboldening us to speak, enlivening our praise with truth, and equipping us with the very words of Jesus.

This means we should expect to see our lives marked with verbal responses to the Spirit's presence. In other words, if we are keeping in step with the Spirit, we will be the kind of people who are compelled to speak often about him to others.

Walking in the Spirit will look like living out loud.

PROLONGING THE INEVITABLE

When we, as believers, suppress spiritual speech, we are only delaying the inevitable. Praise cannot be silenced. The gospel must be preached. Truth will be spoken. It's a matter of *when*, not *if*, the Spirit will lead us to these things. The earth is rumbling with a supernatural compulsion to praise God. When the Holy Spirit moves, spiritual mouths will move.

When Jesus entered Jerusalem the week before his crucifixion, he rode through the streets on a donkey. People from all over town gathered to see him pass by. They marveled at him, and many (probably without even understanding why they were doing it) sang praises to his name. There was a stirring in people's hearts that day. The Holy Spirit was moving in the streets of Jerusalem, and the people were compelled to speak out.

Uncomfortable with this holy rumbling, the religious leaders told Jesus to silence the people. They didn't like being superseded, and they wanted it to stop. But they didn't have eyes to see what was really going on. They thought that thwarting the praise would be as simple as convincing people to shut their mouths. Jesus told them otherwise: "If these were silent, the very stones would cry out."[1] In other words, the praise was inevitable and unstoppable.

Why? Because when the Spirit moves, praise will flow! It is impossible for the name of Jesus not to be glorified and proclaimed when the Spirit is at work. If *we* don't call out praise, the rocks will. Nothing will prevent the sound of praise rising to the Father and the Son. We see a similar reality when Paul says he is compelled to preach the gospel:

> When I preach the gospel, I cannot boast, since I am
> compelled to preach. Woe to me if I do not preach
> the gospel! If I preach voluntarily, I have a reward;
> if not voluntarily, I am simply discharging the trust
> committed to me.
>
> 1 CORINTHIANS 9:16-17, NIV

This passage doesn't directly say that Paul was moved by the Spirit. However, it's clear that something so powerful was happening within him that (from his own perspective) he didn't have a choice. He had to speak. He could have submitted and spoken voluntarily, or he could have spoken involuntarily. Whether he preferred to stay silent doesn't seem to matter. When the Holy Spirit calls us to preach, preaching is inevitable.

What if our lives were so committed to the movement of the

Spirit that even when we didn't want to do or say something, we would be compelled by the power of the Spirit to do it anyway, despite ourselves? What if the Spirit's movement was more compelling in our lives than fear, intimidation, social norms, and our ability to articulate?

Because we know that the gospel will be preached, and Jesus will be praised, with or without us, what if instead of forestalling the inevitable, we welcomed it? As D. L. Moody put it, "When a man is filled with the Word of God you cannot keep him still. If a man has got the Word, he must speak or die."[2]

NOT ALWAYS OUR WORDS

The thing about the Spirit is that he will work in ways we wouldn't on our own. Sometimes we may feel called to say something that seems outlandish. We might have to commit a social faux pas or go out on a limb in a conversation. When we walk in the Spirit, we should expect that sometimes he will have words of his own that he simply intends to use our mouths to say.

In Acts 6 and 7, Stephen is speaking before the Sanhedrin, having been brought up on false charges. As the members of the council listened to him, they "saw that his face was like the face of an angel."[3] We don't know exactly what this means, but I think it points to Stephen's intimacy with God. He had such a close walk with the Holy Spirit that people could actually see it in his countenance. He *looked* like he was filled with the Holy Spirit.

It was out of that same intimacy with the Spirit that Stephen spoke. He was on trial for his life (as it turned out), yet the Holy Spirit led him to say things that were pretty counterintuitive for a guy in his circumstances.

In this interaction with the religious leaders, it seemed like things were starting to go well; it seemed like Stephen was winning them to his side with his knowledge of the Word. But just when the leaders were starting to warm to hearing about Jesus, Stephen says some things that change the entire mood.

"You stiff-necked people! Your hearts and ears are still uncircumcised. You are just like your ancestors: You always resist the Holy Spirit!"[4]

Predictably, the members of the Sanhedrin didn't like that.

As I read this, I wonder if Stephen was questioning himself. Maybe he was shocked at the words coming out of his mouth. Maybe he was surprised by his own boldness. Maybe he saw that things weren't going his way, but he still felt compelled to speak.

This account in Acts teaches us that the Spirit sometimes moves in ways that seem strange. Sometimes he will lead us to say things that don't make a whole lot of earthly sense. Speaking out of obedience to the Spirit may even result in consequences for us. But when we walk in step with the Spirit, and when our words flow out of our intimacy with him, we will say what he compels us to say—no matter the cost.

OPEN YOUR MOUTH AND PRAY

My friend Elise was traveling a while back. She was sitting on a plane when she felt the Holy Spirit prompt her to pray for the woman next to her. She didn't know anything about the woman, and she wasn't accustomed to approaching strangers on an airplane to pray for them. It was clearly out of the ordinary.

Elise wrestled with the idea for a bit. She was certain that the

Holy Spirit was asking her to open her mouth and pray, but she felt uncertain about how to do it.

Finally, she decided that she would allow the Spirit's movement to be more compelling in her life than fear, intimidation, and social norms. So even though she really didn't want to interrupt the woman, she felt compelled to let the Holy Spirit move her mouth. She turned to the woman and said, "Would it be all right if I prayed for you?" And it turned out, the woman sitting next to Elise was on her way to visit her dad, who had just had major surgery. She really needed (and welcomed) the prayer. She and Elise talked for the rest of the flight, and the woman shared about her background and beliefs. They exchanged numbers, kept in touch, and later became friends. That doesn't happen every time, of course, but what if Elise had decided to keep her mouth shut because the situation was a little bit awkward at first?

Stories such as this one of the Spirit moving are not exceptions to the rule. Elise did not experience a rare, once-in-a-lifetime effect of the Holy Spirit in action. When we align ourselves with the Spirit, his voice and ours work in tandem every day. He moves us to engage people. He will lead us to pray for someone, or ask a question, or share a story of his work in our lives. The same Spirit that softens people's hearts and opens their ears is equipping us to engage those hearts and speak to those ears. This is the inevitable, inescapable result of walking in the Spirit. As J. I. Packer put it, "The Holy Spirit is truly God the evangelist."[5]

Christians can spend a good deal of time avoiding evangelism because it feels like a duty, often results in discouragement, and seems to produce very little fruit. But if we begin to grasp the biblical idea of living out loud—allowing the Holy Spirit to speak through us wherever and whenever he chooses—we will evangelize without even realizing it. The Bible shows us that we live out loud as new spiritual people in a landscape of harvestable fields by casting seeds every which way through the power of the Holy Spirit. And then we get to see the unveiling of the exciting story of what God will do.

PRACTICALLY SPEAKING

The Great Commission is not an option to be considered;
it is a command to be obeyed.

HUDSON TAYLOR

LET'S RECAP WHERE WE'VE BEEN SO FAR: Loving God will lead to speaking about God. If we really embrace who we are as new creations in Christ, it will lead to our speaking about God. If we believe the harvest is plentiful, it will lead to our speaking about God. If we take our cues from the farmer in the parable of the sower, it will lead to our speaking about God. And if we walk in the Spirit, it will lead to our speaking about God.

We hope by now you are convinced that God's plan for you, as a new creation, is that you will continually be living out loud and speaking about him. But even if you're sold on the idea of incorporating spiritual things into your everyday language, you might also be asking, "How do I do that?"

The best place to start is where we began—with the Shema.

Hear, O Israel: The LORD our God, the LORD is one. You
shall love the LORD your God with all your heart and
with all your soul and with all your might. And these
words that I command you today shall be on your heart.
You shall teach them diligently to your children, and shall
talk of them when you sit in your house, and when you
walk by the way, and when you lie down, and when you
rise. You shall bind them as a sign on your hand, and they
shall be as frontlets between your eyes. You shall write
them on the doorposts of your house and on your gates.

DEUTERONOMY 6:4-9

These six verses have influenced the way many missionaries
engage people spiritually. From this passage, some missionaries
have developed the term *Shema statements*.[1] A Shema statement is
anything we say that distinguishes us as followers of God. These
are simple, everyday statements that come from our personal walk
with Jesus. They are born out of what we are thinking, what God
is teaching us, how we look at certain situations, what we are wrestling through, what we are reading, or how we are feeling. In other
words, they are the natural things we would say as spiritual people
if we didn't feel the need to hide our spirituality.

Think of these statements as phylacteries—like the little leather
boxes containing the Shema that a Jewish man might wear on his
forehead when he prays. These spiritual statements are things we
say that make it clear to others that we are spiritual people. They
are just as obvious as physical things that we might wear.

"Look at that beautiful sunset. God must be trying to get our
attention."

"You know, I was just praying about that the other day."

"I just really believe God has a plan in mind."

Just like the little leather boxes, these statements aren't hidden; they're obvious.

Using Shema statements is the most natural and practical way I have found to engage people spiritually. It shouldn't be drudgery. The idea isn't to fill a quota of daily statements about God. This is the Shema—where listening becomes doing, where love begets action, where knowing about God and having his words at the tip of our tongues go hand in hand.

"Okay," someone might say, "but Shema statements are not the gospel, they're not enough for a person to *know* Christ." If that's what you're thinking right now, you're right. Shema statements do not necessarily explain the good news of Jesus. However, they do lay the groundwork. Shema statements open the door for the gospel. One of the biggest reasons people give for not sharing the gospel is that they don't know how to bridge the conversation to get there. A lifestyle of living out loud, of using Shema statements, is the bridge. The truth is, people who live out loud and make Shema statements end up explaining the fullness of the gospel far more often than those who do not, and it happens naturally and comfortably.

DISMANTLE THE FILTER

The best way to begin speaking Shema statements is to learn to recognize the spiritual thoughts you have (but suppress) during the day and then give yourself permission to stop biting your tongue. Learn to open your mouth and let the overflow of your heart speak. You love the Lord your God with all your heart; therefore, talk about him all the time.

Let's say a man was in the habit of eating four desserts a day. He wants to become healthier, so he decides to start eating vegetables, too. But if he doesn't lay off the desserts and just adds veggies to his diet, he will not become a healthy eater. The habitual dessert intake has to stop.

The same is true for our language. If we want to learn how to live out loud, and we currently filter out spiritual words, the answer is not to add a few memorized spiritual statements to our conversations. We haven't begun to live out loud until we've stopped habitually suppressing our spirituality. This may seem like semantics, but it's actually the difference between strategizing and living.

Take note of when you tend to filter out spiritual statements from your speech. Maybe you're talking to a neighbor and you have the thought, *That's exactly what God has been teaching me lately*. But instead of being openly spiritual, you say, "That's exactly what I've been thinking about lately." Or maybe your coworker is sharing about a recent struggle and you remember a time when God comforted you in a similar situation. But instead of telling her what God did in your life, you hide the spiritual parts and simply say something like, "Yeah, I've been there too, and it's tough." When you begin watching for this, you'll notice how much you do it, and you can catch yourself before you start. This is what it looks like to dismantle the filter that prevents us from speaking the Shema. It starts with awareness.

BE YOURSELF

Not all Shema statements will be the same for all people or situations. You and I don't have the same personality, which means we will naturally gravitate toward different types of Shema statements.

That's okay. Living out loud is about expressing our own authentic spirituality through our own authentic ways of speaking the Shema, not copying someone else's approach.

I have a friend who is an enthusiast. She genuinely praises God for nearly everything. Job promotion? "Praise the Lord!" New baby? "Praise the Lord!" Got a great parking spot? "Praise the Lord!" I love my friend, and I love the way she expresses her spirituality, but the second I start shouting, "Praise the Lord," I've lost myself. That's not at all a natural way for me to speak. For her, it's a subtle and genuine Shema statement. For me, it would be forced and contrived.

Over the past few years, God has been showing me that when I read the Bible, it isn't always for myself. Sometimes he gives me something to read for a future conversation. I'm starting to see that normal, everyday happenings often bring a passage or Bible story to mind. So every once in a while my Shema statements spill out as references to Scripture. A while back, I was at the gym and had just finished working out. As I was leaving, I passed by the receptionist and asked how her day was going. She said it was going great. When I asked her why it was so great, she explained that her phone had been missing for days and she had found it earlier that morning.

At that moment I realized, *I have a Bible story for that!* The genuine expression of my spirituality in that moment was to say to her, "Wow! You should gather all your friends and throw a party to celebrate finding your phone." (Okay, in the Bible it was a coin, but the principle is the same.)

It was no surprise that my awkward Scripture reference flew right over her head. But as our conversation continued, I explained the Bible story to her. When I told her it was actually a story about someone who was far from God and came to him, and all the angels celebrated the lost person being found, she paused for a moment and then said, "You know, I have never been to church, and I have never read the Bible. But for some strange reason about three weeks ago, I had this desire to buy a Bible, and so I did." I asked her whether she thought God was leading her to read the Bible, and she responded, "I guess so; I bought one!"

We had a great conversation that easily led to spiritual things because of an authentic Shema statement. The original statement, however, never would have made it onto a list of phrases to memorize: "If someone finds something they lost, try mentioning the parable of the lost coin from Luke 15." It wasn't eloquent or well-timed. It was a bit clumsy coming out of my mouth. But it was what came to mind for me as a person who loves God and is working to make him part of my everyday language. And God used it to guide us into a deeper conversation about the Bible and faith.

This is why I can't give you a list of Shema statements to memorize and send you on your way. But I can tell you that as you practice living out loud, you will start to recognize natural Shema statements for yourself. At first it might feel like you really have to search for something spiritual to say, but the more you practice living in light of who you are, the more easily Shema statements will flow through your conversations.

IT COULD GET WEIRD

Even though living in light of who you are is an *identity* more than an approach, it takes practice. The Bible is full of passages that begin with a reality check and end with a command for us to live in light of that reality.

Put off your old self, which is being corrupted by its deceitful desires; to be made new in the attitude of your minds; and . . . put on the new self, created to be like God in true righteousness and holiness.
EPHESIANS 4:22-24, NIV

We have not ceased to pray for you, asking that you may be filled with the knowledge of [God's] will in all spiritual wisdom and understanding, so as to walk in a manner worthy of the Lord, fully pleasing to him: bearing fruit in every good work and increasing in the knowledge of God.
COLOSSIANS 1:9-10

You are the light of the world. A city set on a hill cannot be hidden. Nor do people light a lamp and put it under a basket, but on a stand, and it gives light to all in the house. In the same way, let your light shine before others, so that they may see your good works and give glory to your Father who is in heaven.
MATTHEW 5:14-16

Always be prepared to give an answer to everyone who asks you to give the reason for the hope that you have. But do this with gentleness and respect.
1 PETER 3:15, NIV

Talking about God more often will become a lot more natural as you speak more openly about him. The more you live in light of your new identity, the more spontaneously and genuinely the new language will flow. And because it takes practice, it's okay if it gets a little weird along the way.

You might find yourself in a conversation where you cannot think of a good way to express your spirituality. (This is especially true when you first start trying to be more intentional about it.) Sometimes you'll rack your brain and blurt something out that is completely awkward. Learn to laugh at yourself in those moments.

I have an eye condition that doesn't have a cure but needs to be monitored. Every six months or so, the doctor takes pictures of my eyes to measure regression. It's kind of a vulnerable time for me because I have to sit behind a camera with my chin resting on a contraption that pulls my eyelids apart. I can't see myself, but I know I must look like something straight out of a horror film. Have you ever seen those toys that you squeeze and their eyes pop way out of their heads? Picture that.

One day there was a new technician. She wasn't very talkative, and I was wondering what kind of Shema statement I could make as she took the pictures. I felt prompted to engage her spiritually, but I couldn't think of anything to say in a moment like that. Even though nothing good came to mind, I looked at her (with eyes that would scare any small child) and asked, "So do you think my eye condition is because of *my* sin or the sins of my parents?" (I asked her this question because it's the same one the disciples ask Jesus in John 9:2 when they see a man who has been blind from birth.)

The silence was deafening.

After what seemed like an eternity, she glanced up and without even a hint of a smile said, "You'll have to ask the doctor."

Why would I openly admit this to you? Because I want you to know that living out loud is a process. Learning to display your love for God in every context will take time. It won't always be perfect, and it could get weird. But most of the time it won't. Most of the time you will be surprised by how easy it is to let spiritual things flow into your language. When it does get weird or uncomfortable, don't be discouraged. Remember that you are not alone. Every follower of Jesus gets discouraged from time to time, and no follower of Jesus is exempt from this calling. Sometimes, even an awkward interaction can change someone's life.

Think of spiritual speech as a volume knob. Learning to live out loud is like turning up the volume—figuratively, not literally. If right now you almost never speak about spiritual things and can't remember the last time you said anything that resembled a Shema statement, just start looking for opportunities to change your language. Say something to someone that shows you are a spiritual person. This is a little twist of the knob. Ask God to give you ways to authentically express your spirituality while still being yourself. Ask him to show you how you can start using Shema statements in your everyday conversations.

Evangelism becomes a way of life when who we are as new creations becomes obvious to those around us. When they see overtly spiritual people loving the Lord with all our heart, soul, and might, they're bound to take notice. Loving God this way fulfills the mandate Moses gives in Deuteronomy 6:6-7:

> These words that I command you today shall be on your
> heart. You shall teach them diligently to your children,

and shall talk of them when you sit in your house, and
when you walk by the way, and when you lie down, and
when you rise.

Evangelism becomes inevitable when we naturally live out loud
in every context—one Shema statement at a time.

7

ONLY TIME WILL TELL

We must never think that because a nonbeliever remained
unconvinced by our case that our apologetic has failed.
For one encounter is not the end of the story.

WILLIAM LANE CRAIG

JOANNE WAS AN EVANGELISTIC ATHEIST—that is, she was an atheist, and she was evangelistic about it. She wanted to convince everyone around her that there was no God, and she enjoyed mocking anyone who thought otherwise. Joanne was also my colleague (maybe I would even say work friend). She was nice and funny and enjoyable to be around. And mostly I was okay with her picking on me.

If she was standing in a group of other colleagues and I came up, Joanne might say, "Oh, everyone, watch your language; Kevin is here." Or she might say in her playful, mocking way, "Oh, we have to be careful because God might see us." Or my personal favorite, "Kevin, what are you doing with your God Squad friends this weekend? Having a wild prayer meeting party?" As Joanne would tease, I would just smile and sometimes even laugh. Sometimes, her joking at my expense was just plain funny. Other times, it was annoying, and I would say, "Ha ha, funny, Joanne," and roll my eyes.

That was the kind of friendship we had. Joanne would tease, and I would try to live out my spirituality without crumbling under her persistent pressure. There wasn't any real tension, but this was how things went year after year. Then one morning, when Joanne came into work, she passed by all her friends and coworkers without a word, and ignoring her own office door, walked straight into my office and sat down.

Before I could say a word, her chin began to quiver and her eyes filled with tears.

"Can you pray for my mother? I just found out last night that she has cancer, and I'm really scared!"

"Of course I will."

I prayed for Joanne and her mother with strong compassion. But after she left my office, I couldn't help but wonder, *What just happened?* The unlikeliest person to ask for prayer—indeed, the very last person I ever thought would come to me—just had.

When her world turned upside down, Joanne needed someone who could fix broken things, bring joy amid sadness, offer hope when things were crumbling. She needed somewhere to turn in her pain; and despite all odds, she turned to God. I didn't know exactly what was going on or how long it would last, but something had changed for Joanne. And I had the privilege of being there for her in the midst of it.

But in that moment, something also changed for me. It had to. I had written Joanne off spiritually. I had put her name in the "not worth engaging" column. Not consciously, of course. I had still lived out loud with her. But deep down, I had never really expected it to go anywhere. According to my estimation, her heart was too hard. But I couldn't see what God sees. I couldn't account for what was happening beneath the surface. In my arrogance, I had assumed that God shared my estimation, when all along he was in the business of doing things that didn't seem to add up. I was looking at outward appearances. God was looking at the heart.[1]

HARDNESS TODAY DOESN'T MEAN HARDNESS TOMORROW

This is what the kingdom of God is like. A man scatters seed on the ground. Night and day, whether he sleeps or gets up, the seed sprouts and grows, though he does not know how. All by itself the soil produces grain— first the stalk, then the head, then the full kernel in the head. As soon as the grain is ripe, he puts the sickle to it, because the harvest has come.

MARK 4:26-29, NIV

In Mark 4, Jesus tells a parable about a farmer. Picture this farmer in your mind's eye. Spend a minute imagining his farming methods. He scatters some seeds, and then what? How would you describe his demeanor? Is he frantic? Does he seem to spend a lot of time studying the growth patterns of the region and which techniques he could implement for a better harvest? Does he see himself as responsible for what happens? Does he seem desperate, anxious, worried?

He doesn't strike me as the kind of farmer who is losing sleep at night. Once he has scattered the seed, he just goes about his day. I don't get the impression he was constantly worried about whether there would be growth. I also don't think he was surprised by the growth. He seems to be very aware of his role as a farmer and God's role as Creator.

The crazy thing about this parable is that Jesus says this is what it looks like when the Kingdom of God is revealed on earth. As God works and his Kingdom is on display, it will be marked by a slow, steady growth that happens because seeds were planted and God turned them into a harvest. And we should take note that some of that pivotal growth occurs beneath the soil, where we can't see it, measure it, or calculate it.

You've probably caught on to the fact that we're no longer talking about the wheat harvest here. You and I are privileged to do scattering of a different sort—the kind of scattering that happens every time we engage with people spiritually. What if we were to take a cue from the farmer, scatter our seed, and leave the rest up to God? God calls us to speak about him, and then he takes on the responsibility for whatever growth happens next.

The key is to recognize that *all* growth happens because of God's supernatural influence. And that is exactly what I had failed to recognize with Joanne. It didn't matter one bit that she was mocking God on Monday, because on Thursday she called out to him. If all growth is supernatural, then it really doesn't matter how hardened someone appears to be, right? God has his ways.

Think about a dead body. There is nothing you and I can do to change its condition. We could scream at it, kick it, nudge it, or prop it up, but no amount of our effort will ever change its deadness. Dead things can't respond, and we can't make them. This is the imagery Paul uses in his letter to the Ephesians to describe the miraculous, transformative nature of God's power:

> You were dead in the trespasses and sins in which you
> once walked, following the course of this world, following
> the prince of the power of the air, the spirit that is now
> at work in the sons of disobedience—among whom we
> all once lived in the passions of our flesh, carrying out
> the desires of the body and the mind, and were by nature
> children of wrath, like the rest of mankind. But God,
> being rich in mercy, because of the great love with which
> he loved us, even when we were dead in our trespasses,
> made us alive together with Christ.
>
> EPHESIANS 2:1-5

According to Paul, those who haven't been made alive in Christ are dead. And before any of the Ephesian Christians had time to jump on their high horses, Paul reminded them that they, too, had all been dead once. I take this to mean we all have more in common with a corpse than we would like to admit. Every single person whom God has ever brought to new life was first dead in their sins.

This should encourage you. It should encourage you because you are not called to bring dead things to life. God does that. And it should encourage you to see beyond what seems possible or impossible in a person's life. I did not believe the gospel because I was any less dead than Joanne.

You did not believe because you were any less dead than anyone else. Our friends and coworkers will not come to Jesus because they are less dead than others, but because they will be miraculously brought to life. We can never conclude that a person is too dead!

Mark Dever reminds us of this in his book *The Gospel and Personal Evangelism*:

> You and I aren't called to use our extensive powers to
> convict and change the sinner while God stands back
> as a gentleman, quietly waiting for the spiritual corpse,
> his declared spiritual enemy, to invite God into his
> heart. Rather, we should resolve to preach the gospel like
> gentlemen, persuading while knowing we can't regenerate
> anyone, and then stand back while God uses all his
> extensive powers to convict and change the sinner. Then
> we'll see clearly who it is that can really call the dead to
> life, and although he'll use us in the doing of it, it's not
> you and I who are actually doing it.[2]

This is really the only posture we can have if we recognize that God is the one who is doing all the work. We can engage people spiritually and feel the freedom to walk away when they aren't receptive. That isn't "bad evangelism"; it is a wise expression of trust. It is knowing how much is our responsibility—what lies within our power to accomplish—and how much is not. It is being the kind of farmer who sleeps restfully, knowing that personal effort will never be the thing that causes a seed to grow. How much of a difference do you think it would make if the people you engaged no longer sensed desperation and anxiety from you; if instead they found you to be a nonanxious spiritual presence in their lives?

HOSTILITY TODAY DOESN'T MEAN HOSTILITY TOMORROW

Ananias lived in Damascus and was a faithful follower of Jesus. He was the kind of man who heard from God and obeyed him. He also lived in a time of great persecution of Christians. Ananias had heard stories about a man named Saul who would hunt down Christians to kill them. Maybe he even knew someone who had been captured by Saul.

What Ananias didn't know was that Saul was on his way to Damascus to find more Christians. Ananias didn't know this until God told him. But God didn't speak a warning or provide a way of escape. Instead, he told Ananias to find Saul and heal him.

Understandably, Ananias pushed back. He had heard some things, made some calculations, and had decided that Saul's name belonged on the "not worth engaging" list. But Ananias also didn't know that God was at work in Saul's life. God had a plan to make Saul "a chosen instrument . . . to carry my name before the Gentiles and kings and the children of Israel."[3] In other words, it didn't matter one bit that Saul was killing Christians on Monday, because on Thursday he was going to have an encounter with Jesus.

I told you about Joanne, but Saul was definitely the least likely guy *ever* to come to Jesus. Hardened through and through. Not just opposed to Christianity, but trying to wipe it out. Yet that's exactly the type of person God works on. Then and now, God has always loved taking people who seem (and sometimes are) the least likely, most hardened, not-worth-engaging types of people and saving them. Suddenly, where we could have sworn there would never be any growth, something springs up and turns into a ripe harvest.

Keep your conduct among the Gentiles honorable,
so that when they speak against you as evildoers, they
may see your good deeds and glorify God on the day
of visitation.
1 PETER 2:12

Not only will there be times when the ripening is slow, but the
apostle Peter says there will also be times when people are down-
right hostile to our identity as followers of Jesus. But Peter also says
there will be times when that hostility gives way to receptivity. As
we live out our spirituality with consistency as followers of Jesus,
God can use us to change people's hearts. Our obvious life and
language as steady Christ followers will lead them to glorify God.
As Peter puts it, after the slandering is when the good deeds are
noticed. Or in Joanne's case, after all the mocking was when the
prayer happened.

God has people on a journey, and no two individuals come
to him in exactly the same way. When we live out loud, we will
encounter people in many stages of receptivity—some hard as a
rock toward God, some seemingly dry, some with little sprouts,
some bursting with grain—all worth engaging. It is arrogant and
tragic for us to think that we see far enough into people's hearts
that we can deem them "bad soil." And it keeps us turning our
spirituality on and off with every conversation instead of speaking
naturally and consistently. We must remember that we will always
be looking at (and interacting with) dead people until God brings
them to life. In other words, the situation will always look bleak
until God brings hope.

What feels to us like a natural conversation on a normal
Tuesday may actually be the catalyst for something growing

beneath the surface. We never know which moment will be the one when death turns to life. The only way for us to be a part of all of those not-so-normal interactions is if we start scattering seed and trusting God for the growth—no matter who seems too far gone and no matter how long it seems to take. Today's hard case may be tomorrow's new birth. Those mocking us today might be praying with us tomorrow. Those who are persecuting Christians today might be coming to Christ tomorrow. Isn't living in that hope an exhilarating way to spend a Tuesday?

8

DIVINE APPOINTMENTS

*God is the Great Engineer, creating circumstances
to bring about moments in our lives of divine
importance that lead to divine appointments.*

OSWALD CHAMBERS

IMAGINE THAT AS YOU ARE WALKING down the street on
your way to work, you have a strong impression that you should
take a different route than you normally would. You veer to the
right, hang a left, and suddenly you encounter someone who is
reading a Bible and who asks if you could answer some questions.
How exciting would that moment be? To have a sense that God
spoke to you, you heard him correctly, and he used you to speak
to someone else—it doesn't get much better than that!

That is exactly the kind of moment Philip has in Acts 8:26-39
as he walks along the desert road from Jerusalem toward Gaza.
He senses God telling him to go south, and along the way he
runs into an Ethiopian official who is reading aloud from the

book of Isaiah.* Philip asks the man if he understands what he is reading, and that question starts a conversation that culminates in the first recorded Ethiopian conversion and baptism. Not only that, but some of the earliest Christian presence in Africa can be traced to Ethiopia—and some believe it can be attributed to this very man.

If you were to look at a religious map of Africa down through history, you would notice that Islam has held sway over the north for centuries. Even today, country after country is majority Muslim. But there is one outlier, one country where the gospel has had a continual presence. That country is Ethiopia.

Can you imagine how incredible it would be if a simple moment of obedience led you to participate in a divine appointment that brought someone to Jesus? For some, this is a recurring scenario. For others, it feels like the sort of thing that would never happen. As my friend Anna told me, for her it was a matter of overcoming fear:

> I wanted God to use me. I wanted epic encounters and great moments. I wanted to be on the front lines as people realized hope for the first time. But it always felt like a thing other people got to do. Either they knew something I didn't, or they were braver than I was, or they had the gift of evangelism that seemed to skip me. That was one part of my fear.

---

* The text says that "an angel of the Lord" said to Philip that he should head south, but it doesn't tell us *how* the angel said this to him. Whenever God, one of his angelic messengers, or the Holy Spirit speaks to us, we might hear his voice audibly in a way that others nearby could also hear. We might hear it loud and clear in our own mind, but others would not be able to hear it. Or we might have an impression so strong that we feel confident God is directing us (I think this is how most people experience the voice of the Lord). But in all three cases, we might say, "The Lord told me to do this or that."

The other part was that I didn't want to have bad interactions. I was afraid of being one of those ridiculous Christians who corner people with the gospel. I thought if I was awkward, or misread the moment, I would actually do more harm than good. Like if people encountered me, they might accidentally end up further away from Jesus because I made him look bad.

That was the tension I lived in for a long time. Mostly, it left me crippled. Mostly, I erred on the side of saying nothing so as not to say the wrong thing. The one thing I could say with confidence was that I wasn't having awkward interactions that made God look bad, but it was only because I was having no interactions that pointed people to Jesus.

One day I was with a friend who was telling me about her new goal. She wanted to try to share the gospel with at least three people every week. My first thought was cynical. Putting some weird quota on it was certain to lead to forced interactions. Her plan would definitely leave a bad taste in people's mouths.

"What about Saturday night when you haven't met your goal and you go find the first unsuspecting person and shove the gospel down their throat? Don't you think that will be a bad way to share Jesus with someone?"

I thought I had her.

She smiled and responded with a simple logic that would turn out to wreak havoc on my life.

"God is the Giver of divine appointments. If he knows I'm going out on a Saturday night looking for someone, don't you think he would bring the right someone along? And if he does, there will be no need to be forceful."

I was so jealous of the freedom she seemed to have. She didn't bear the weight of possibly ruining people spiritually like I did. Her confidence in God's ability to orchestrate supernatural moments lifted that weight from her shoulders. What's more, she lived smack-dab in the middle of all the action I longed for. That began a wrestling in me, and in the following weeks God chipped away at my misperceptions.

I didn't implement a weekly goal (though I no longer believe that to be a bad idea), but I did start to see God as the giver of divine appointments. I started living with the assumption that he was working and that I was invited to be a part of it. I felt the freedom to have awkward conversations because I believed God could see my awkwardness coming from a mile away and had every opportunity to prepare that person for it.

And as I engaged people, I was surprised by how little power I had to ruin them spiritually. It turns out God isn't at the mercy of my performance—whether I'm being cool enough, relevant enough, or intriguing enough. He is capable of drawing people to himself despite me. If he is orchestrating moments and inviting me to be a part of them, he probably isn't afraid of me messing them up.

Perhaps you find yourself in a similar place as Anna. Maybe you've wondered why God seems to use others and not you. Maybe you read stories of the early church and wish that God would show up in the same incredible ways he did so long ago. Maybe you wish your track record looked a whole lot more like Philip's.

Scripture makes it clear that God indeed orchestrates divine appointments in at least some instances, for some people. But if we are longing for these things, why does it seem that his supernatural hand of appointment skips over us?

On a practical and experiential level, I've found that people who consistently live out loud seem to get divine appointments when other believers do not. It could be that God reserves these moments for people he knows will be faithful with them. Or it could be that God gives divine appointments to every believer, but only some recognize them and respond. Whatever the case, if you and I are speaking openly about our love for God, we will experience more divine appointments than if we're keeping our mouths shut.

There are some who (due to silence) will sit on the sidelines and watch others celebrate the joys of the harvest. They'll wonder why those other people always seem to find the fruit, and they'll wish God would give them some divine appointments of their own. It may never occur to them that they are simply missing the opportunities that God provides. They'll be like the crowd in Matthew 25:44 who say to Jesus, "Lord, when did we see you hungry or thirsty or a stranger or naked or sick or in prison, and did not minister to you?" In other words, they will be oblivious to the many opportunities God brings for all of us to join him in his work.

DON'T MISS OUT

We don't have to miss out. We can be among those who recognize and take advantage of the opportunities all around us. For those who relate more easily with the crowd in Matthew 25:44 than with Philip on the desert road, let me offer a few practical thoughts:

1. Pray for divine appointments

If you'd like to see more of the opportunities God brings, ask him to make you more aware. Prayer has the ability to draw our attention away from the mundane and into the supernatural. Ask God to bring you divine appointments, and then watch for them.

2. Anticipate divine appointments

As we approach conversations with people, we can assume God is working and proceed as if we believe in divine interventions. As Jim Elliff, founder and president of Christian Communicators Worldwide, has said,

> We have not made enough of the fact that evangelism has a great deal to do with what you *expect* God to do. If you raise your antennae as the day begins and ask God to make you an instrument for divine encounters during the day, it will happen—almost every time. Christians living in anticipation of being used by God are like cats on the lookout for mice. They never lose their focus. They seem to sleep with their eyes and ears alert. When you stay ready, you are actually living by the faith you claim to exercise![1]

3. Pursue divine appointments

If you think God is telling you to veer right and hang a left, do it. Practice obedience. As you practice following God's prompting in your life, you will become more sensitive to his leading. You'll recognize his voice and develop a rapport of trust.

You and I will most certainly miss every opportunity we talk ourselves out of pursuing, but we just might find that divine appointments arrive on the heels of our obedience.

4. Speak in divine appointments

If you let your love for God flow into your everyday language, divine appointments will not pass you by. The Shema isn't a gimmick or a technique; it is God's design for our lives, and it happens to be the answer to so many of our nagging questions. If we create a rhythm of speaking about God, we will automatically make the most of divine appointments.

5. Trust God with your divine appointments

It can be scary to pray for and anticipate divine appointments when you're wondering whether God will give you more than you can handle. Maybe the thought of engaging someone on your commute to work sounds exhausting. Maybe you can't imagine having the time to pour into one more person right now. Remember that God holds time in his hands. Remember that he isn't asking you to do anything by your own strength. Divine appointments aren't for the good of the unbeliever at the expense of the believer. Trust that God knows what he is doing when he brings people your way.

YUSUF AND THE AMERICAN CHRISTIAN

Yusuf grew up in a very religious family. His father was an imam, and Yusuf followed in his footsteps. Day after day, Yusuf performed the religious services, but he silently struggled with what felt to him like a heavy burden of rules and expectations. As he read the Koran looking for answers, he found only more uncertainty.

Eventually, this internal battle led Yusuf to step down from his role as imam. When he did, his family rejected him, his fiancée broke off their engagement, and Yusuf found himself in a downward spiral. Depressed and alone, he was contemplating suicide when he decided to cry out to God for help. He began praying, "God, whoever you are, I don't care, please just help me and show me what to do."

Shortly after that desperate prayer, Yusuf had a dream in which God spoke to him, saying, "The truth you are seeking will be found in New York City. Move there."

In obedience, Yusuf moved to New York City and entered a graduate program there. He saw a flyer on campus inviting students to one of our team's English conversation groups, and he decided to go. After the first group meeting, he and Chris (the group leader) went to lunch. Chris asked Yusuf what had brought him to New York, and without knowing that Chris was a believer, Yusuf explained his journey.

When Yusuf was done, Chris responded very simply, "I believe the truth you are seeking is found in Jesus. Would you like to study the Bible together?"

As Yusuf began reading the Bible looking for answers, he found certainty. He believed it to be the real answer from God.

Merriam-Webster lists two common meanings for the word *divine*. The first refers to something "proceeding directly from God." The second refers to something "supremely good."[2]

Two common meanings of the word *appointment* are "an arrangement for a meeting" and "an act of appointing someone" to a task.[3]

Long before Chris and Yusuf's interaction, God was directing their steps. Through Yusuf's days as an imam, through dreams, through his moving to a new place—and even through a flyer—God was orchestrating something in Yusuf's life. And long before Chris ever knew it, God was planning to use him to draw a man out of a Muslim country, into his conversation group, and out to lunch so Chris could introduce him to Jesus. It seems to me that God was carefully planning excellent ways to introduce himself to Yusuf by appointing Chris to engage him. That kind of planning—crossing oceans, spanning years, and abounding in nuance—can only be called one thing: a divine appointment.

God is on the move. He is orchestrating encounters and preparing hearts for engagement. We don't need to spend our lives on the sidelines wondering why everyone else seems to get the opportunities we don't. If we are embracing the Shema—living out loud as people of God—we can expect that God will divinely place spiritually hungry people in proximity to us. And with our eyes open to the possibilities and our mouths flowing with love for God, we will be ready to make the most of those appointments when they come.

9

COLLATERAL IMPACT

Stop regarding all the unpleasant things as interruptions
of one's "own," or "real" life. The truth is . . . that
what one calls the interruptions are precisely one's
real life—the life God is sending one day by day.

C. S. LEWIS

RYAN WAS ON one of our ministry teams. He lived in an area
of New York that was home to more than one hundred thousand
West African Muslims. One day, Ryan was in a bodega (that's the
NYC word for "corner store"; it makes us feel fancy), and he was
talking with a West African Muslim man about the gospel. As he
was showing the man some things from the New Testament, a
West African woman walked past, stopped, and then asked the
men what they were discussing. Ryan said they were talking about
Jesus, and the woman asked if she could talk with Ryan next.

After Ryan finished his first conversation, the woman intro-
duced herself as Sandrine. She went on to share that she was a
Christian but had never known how to reach her people with
the gospel. She had felt a calling to talk to others about God but

never knew what it could look like, and she had been praying that God would help her. When she overheard Ryan's conversation, Sandrine knew God was answering her prayers.

Ryan thought he was just sharing the gospel with a man in a bodega, but God had been stirring another heart as well. After meeting Sandrine that day, Ryan and his wife began to disciple and train her. She grew in her faith and became more and more passionate about sharing the good news of Jesus with others.

Eventually, God called Sandrine to move back to her home country, where she could tell her friends and family about Jesus. Sandrine is from the Wolof people group in Senegal. The Wolof are 99 percent Muslim and considered an unreached people group. Foreign missionaries have made very little progress in engaging them. But Sandrine knew she could make an impact there. She moved back and started a house church that is still flourishing today. Every week, she engages people and reaches places we could never go. And it all started with an overheard conversation.

A LESSON FROM NEW YORK

The word *collateral* often connotes unintended side effects. For example, we use the phrase "collateral damage" when civilians are unintentional casualties of war. But when it comes to spiritual engagement, what may be unintentional on our part is fully intentional on God's part. As he did with Ryan, he may prompt us to speak to one person for the sake of someone else who happens to overhear. I call this *collateral impact*. Our conversations have the potential to ripple out in ways that affect people we don't even know and never had in mind.

True fact: There are more people in New York City than there is space to put them. Our apartments are notoriously small. Subways and elevators are packed. Lines are long. And restaurants are so crowded that you could reach over and eat from a stranger's plate without even straightening your elbow. This was a bit of a shock when I first moved into my neighborhood and found myself over-hearing every conversation. Suddenly I knew what strangers were cooking for dinner and planning for the weekend and whether or not they liked what was playing in the theaters.

Knowing that my own conversations were also on display made me shy away from living out loud. In the moments when I would say something spiritual, I found myself sort of whispering it so as not to be overheard. Even still, people would say things like, "Excuse me. I couldn't help but overhear you say . . ."

As more and more of those secondary conversations began leading to opportunities, I started to realize that God had more in mind for my conversations than I did. I started to recognize the potential for collateral impact, and it liberated me from my fear-driven whispering.

There is something to be said for living in an environment where privacy is a luxury. It has a way of rooting out our timidity. But more important, it forces us to see that God is working in greater ways than we may recognize. You may not live in one of the five boroughs of NYC—forced by proximity to air all your private concerns in public—but the lesson is the same for everyone: We may be focused on having conversations with the person in front of us, but there is often more going on in our periphery.

My friend Steven was in Queens talking with someone about God. They were in a public area, and as they spoke, a Tibetan man walked by (because it's New York). Overhearing their conversation (again, because it's New York), he apologized for interrupting, and said, "Last night I had a dream. I saw Jesus coming down out of the clouds, and he was pointing at me. Can you tell me what my dream means?"

Steven responded by saying he didn't know exactly what the dream meant, but it seemed clear that God wanted him to know Jesus.

Before his conversation with Steven, this Tibetan man didn't know much about who Jesus is, but God had been stirring his heart. In fact, God was pursuing him so intently that he appeared to him in a dream. Not only that, but he prompted Steven to engage someone else in a spiritual conversation at the very moment the man was walking by. Because of his unintentional eavesdropping, this Tibetan man heard the gospel that day for the first time in his life. And because God had already been working in his heart, he received Christ that same day.

> So shall my word be that goes out from my mouth; it
> shall not return to me empty, but it shall accomplish
> that which I purpose, and shall succeed in the thing for
> which I sent it.
> ISAIAH 55:11

God knows what he is doing, and he is incredibly effective at it. His Word goes where he wants it to go and accomplishes what he wants it to accomplish. As we engage people spiritually, here are two ways we can think through Isaiah 55:11: On the one hand, it might mean that every time God prompts us to engage someone spiritually, his Word is affecting them even if we can't see it. On the other hand, it might mean that every time God prompts us to engage someone, his Word is accomplishing something, even if it isn't for the specific person we thought it was for. These may be two sides of the same coin.

In our humanness, we can't account for the supernatural. We might never see things like collateral impact coming. And the beauty of it is that we don't need to. God has made us into new creations and invites us to live out that newness in obvious ways. We just get to be along for the exciting ride as he does more than we expected and often different things than we intended.

EVEN IN THE GROCERY STORE

Kenny definitely got more than he expected as he walked into the grocery store one day and noticed an old acquaintance on the other side of the store. He would have happily gone about his shopping, but he felt God leading him to go say hello. They greeted each other, and (true to form) Kenny let his love for God flow into the conversation as they spoke. As the conversation continued, Kenny could sense that his friend was resistant to what he shared. When they went their separate ways, Kenny wasn't sure what to make of it. He assumed God was doing something, but what?

As he began shopping, he wondered why God had prompted that interaction with someone whose heart seemed hardened. Then, as he walked down another aisle, a woman approached him and said, "I was in the next aisle over and was able to hear your conversation. I apologize for listening, but when you were talking with your friend, I felt like God was speaking directly to me."

Suddenly, Kenny was no longer wondering why God had prompted him. As he had conversed, every word had floated over shelves filled with cereal boxes and canned beans and into the ears of someone who needed to hear what Kenny was saying. God's word went out and did not return empty. And Kenny had done his part without even knowing it.

Ryan's and Kenny's stories make me wonder how much I have missed along the way. How often have I walked away feeling as if a conversation was pointless? Maybe God was doing more than I realized. How often have I focused only on the person in front of me? Maybe God was stirring the heart of someone else. How often have I lowered my voice so as not to be overheard? Maybe the person two tables away needed to hear my conversation.

If God is the one moving, we should anticipate that speaking as spiritual people will result in collateral impact. When we let our language reflect our love for God, there will be times when our conversations ripple out into ears we could have never known were listening. We can't know what's happening under the surface, or how the words will be used to bring dead things to life, or who will be receptive and who won't, or how long it will take, or even who might be overhearing. But we can allow God's goodness to be on the tips of our tongues, and we can speak freely as followers of Jesus. We can meet people and authentically and genuinely display our spirituality.

So let's leave the strategizing up to God. He's far better at it than we are. Only God can bring two West Africans—one a Muslim, the other a Christian—into a corner store at just the right moment. Only God can give a Tibetan man dreams and a conversation to overhear in New York City. Only God can send a woman down the right grocery aisle to find what she didn't know she was looking for. God has told us to love him with all that we are, and he has called us to live as new creations. And if we do, he will use us to accomplish so much more than we could ever imagine.

SELLING JESUS

A rule I have had for years is to treat the Lord Jesus Christ as a personal friend. It is not a creed, a mere empty doctrine, but it is Christ Himself we have.

DWIGHT L. MOODY

SOMETHING STRANGE IS HAPPENING in the church. We have unwittingly turned Jesus into something we sell, or a topic of debate, rather than the person that we know. This tendency has skewed our ideas of what it means to engage people and has actually become a distraction from fruitful evangelism.

It isn't malicious; it's just that we have jobs in sales and marketing and product development, and we've been conditioned to think like consumers. Thus we have become accustomed to the idea of Jesus as a product. We also live in a world of debates and social media and soapboxes, and thus we have become accustomed to the idea of Jesus as a position to defend. But if we are going to be effective at introducing people to Jesus, we can't devolve him into a product or a position; we must treat him as the person he is.

JESUS AS A PRODUCT

If we try to sell Jesus as a product, it will lead us into two traps that keep us from being authentic. First, we will tend to oversell Christianity, making it seem to be something it's not. Second, we will feel the need to hide our imperfections as Christians, so as not to discredit Jesus. Both of these will hinder us from living out loud.

I have never had a job in advertising, but I have been the target of advertising millions of times. So have you. In fact, the average American sees somewhere between four thousand and ten thousand ads every single day.[1] To someone who knows what it means to be bombarded with product promotions, it seems that the number one goal of advertising is to make something look good; make it appealing; show the audience that it's going to improve their lives in some way. The most common way that ads accomplish this is by overselling.

"This new shampoo doesn't just smell good; it's also going to make your hair the envy of all your friends and neighbors and coworkers. With wonderful hair like that, your complexion will look better, your clothes will look better, and eventually you will probably become famous."

Now, before you hear me wrong, I know you can't oversell Jesus. You can't overstate his goodness, overemphasize what he accomplished on our behalf, or exaggerate his holiness. But we most certainly can oversell the Christian life. And we do. We say to people, "Everything in my life is perfect because of Jesus, and he can make everything in your life perfect too." End of commercial.

Allow me to let you off the hook: Jesus doesn't need us to say things like that.

There are entire sections of Scripture dedicated to the struggles of walking with God. David cries out with unanswered prayers and feelings of distance between him and God. The same goes for Solomon, Job, Jonah, Hosea, Paul—just about every believer from the Old and New Testaments. The Bible doesn't sugarcoat what it means to follow Jesus, and we don't have to either. Of course our lives are new and different because of Jesus. And of course we can say with authenticity that he has brought joy and hope like we never knew before we met him. But that's not the whole picture.

Jesus himself said that following him will look like dying on a cross.[2] He promised that it would be hard and we would be stretched. But somehow, supernaturally, dying to ourselves is where we truly find life. Somehow with Jesus, joy and suffering are not mutually exclusive. We need to let those beautifully profound truths stand on their own merits and not try to slap a veneer of perfection over them. Our Shema statements can reveal both the hardship and the fulfillment of walking with Jesus.

Not only should we be honest about the cost of following Jesus, but we should also be honest about how we have failed at it. If our goal is to *sell* Jesus, it's a really bad marketing strategy to be open about our struggles as his followers. I have never seen a commercial where the spokesperson talked about forgetting to use the product, or how the product doesn't seem to be meeting her needs, or how the product hasn't answered her prayers in a while. If we were selling Jesus, honesty and transparency would not be helpful.

But it's a great way to live out loud.

Thankfully, Jesus isn't a product, and he doesn't need to be sold. He is a person who needs to be known. This means that even our struggles can become Shema statements. Even saying that we feel like God is far away, even being honest about not getting much out of Scripture lately, even speaking about how hard it is to submit to Jesus, even all of our struggles can be ways that we live out loud with the people around us.

There is a pastor who lives down the street from me. Whenever someone asks how he is doing, he responds with, "Too blessed to be stressed. Blessed by the best." This isn't bad, or even inauthentic, but I'm willing to bet that sometimes he actually is stressed. People can see through the facade of perfection, and it's not appealing. Tell me a shampoo smells good, and I'll probably believe you. Tell me it will make me famous, and I'm no longer listening.

The really good news is that God draws people to himself, and he can use your pain just as much as he can use your joy. Talking about answered prayers or unanswered prayers are both forms of spiritual engagement. Tell a neighbor about your disappointments as a Christian. Strike up a conversation about your neighbor's disappointments with Jesus. You never know who might need to hear the authenticity of your struggle before they will let down their guard.

We don't have to pad our stories and speak in clichés, because Jesus isn't a product, and we aren't in charge of making him marketable. We just need to let our walk with Jesus spill out into our conversations in ways that reflect where we really are in that walk.

JESUS AS A POSITION

You don't have to look too far in our culture to find opinions. They are everywhere. In our social-media-saturated society, it seems that Americans by and large feel a sense of obligation to live from soapbox to soapbox. We think everyone needs to know where we stand on any given issue, and we know just how to get the word out. This contributes, I think, to the tendency of some Christians to see following Jesus as a position to take and defend rather than as a relationship with a real person.

We have reduced "spiritual engagement" to posting something controversial on social media or getting into an argument about morality. We might even feel that we have "done our evangelistic duty" by taking a stance against injustice or calling out unrighteousness. And if Jesus were a *position*, these might be incredibly effective ways to defend him. But they are very ineffective ways to engage people spirituality and introduce them to the *person* of Jesus.

I was speaking at a church recently about living out loud. After my talk, a woman came up to me and thanked me, saying, "This was so inspiring, and now I realize I have been too quiet about my faith." I was encouraged to think that my talk may have influenced her to turn up her spiritual volume. Then she continued, "My sister isn't a believer, and her daughter is gay. I've been silent, but now I'm going to let her know my views about homosexuality." I realized then that she had heard me all wrong. In her mind, turning up the volume meant being more vocal about moral positions. In the gentlest way I could, I tried to explain that this was not what I meant.

The thing is, sharing political persuasions, defending positions, and even telling people our ideas about morality are not synonymous with engaging people spiritually. We are not primarily conservative or liberal or free-thinking or moralistic. We are primarily *new*. To live the Shema is to *speak about God as people who love God*; it is not to hold positions or enter debates on God's behalf. That doesn't mean it's bad for us to have positions or take stances, but we can't fool ourselves into calling it evangelism. As Timothy Keller said, "Bad evangelism says: I'm right, you're wrong, and I would love to tell you about it."[3]

When we look at the life of Jesus, he almost never chose to introduce himself to people by taking a stance on a position. Instead, he met them in the middle of their sin and allowed them to encounter his love and grace. When the teachers of the law were about to stone the woman caught in adultery, they stated their position on the law and the prescribed penalty. Maybe they thought by taking a stance they were displaying God's holiness.

But what did Jesus do? He responded with love and grace. That doesn't mean he ignored the sin. In fact, he called the woman to repent from it—"and from now on sin no more."[4] But in every situation, his prevailing posture and strongest stance as he engaged people was love and grace. Debating people into new thinking is so far from the heart of Jesus that we see him actively avoiding it. Instead of debating, Jesus was much more likely to ask a thought-provoking question or tell a story for those who had ears to hear.[5]

As we engage people, we should be aware of our propensity to make it about our opinions when it is always about the person of Jesus. Ask any one of your neighbors, and they will probably have stories to tell you about how opinionated Christians have rubbed them the wrong way. In fact, that's a good way to engage your neighbors in spiritual conversations. Let them talk about their frustrations with Jesus as a position, and then try to introduce them to Jesus as a person. We need to stop having the wrong conversations. We don't need to change people's minds; we serve a God who can actually change their hearts.

JESUS AS A PERSON

About two thousand years ago, a man who was like no other walked the earth. He left a heavenly throne to step into our world and walk among us. He was the God of the universe experiencing the fullness of being human. His life changed everything about what it means to live, and his death changed everything about what it means to die. In his resurrection, he established a Kingdom that alters our citizenship, awakens our joy, and brings us real hope. To know him is to know the truth, and to submit to him is to be truly free. He offers us not only life but himself as the means to it. It is through a relationship with him that we are made new and we learn to flourish in our humanity.

The exciting thing about living out loud spiritually is that it opens the door for people to know Jesus. To attempt to sell him would be to cheapen him. To make morality the issue puts the cart before the horse. In the midst of a loudly opinionated, consumerist culture, how refreshing it is to encounter something greater than all that noise! Every simple conversation where we allow God to saturate our words can become the means by which someone comes to trust, love, and follow Jesus—to know him not merely as a reasonable conclusion to a theological proposition but as our deeply relational Lord and Savior.

God reveals himself in a personal way through Scripture. He could have condensed everything into a few simple statements about who he is and what that means for us. He could have laid out a bullet-point gospel, provided a theological outline, and given us a list of commands to follow. Instead, he chose to reveal himself through stories. Over thousands of years, through relational narratives and the lives of people who knew him, he showed us his character. Through people's failures and victories, through their poems and prayers, he taught us how to walk with him.

God also revealed himself in a personal way through Jesus. He inhabited our human life, walked among us, and showed us what he was like in tangible ways. He invited a group of disciples into a close, personal relationship with him and demonstrated the power of love, faith, and obedience. As the disciples journeyed with Jesus day by day, he taught them how to live. Through parables and miracles, in daily rhythms and life decisions, he showed us all what it means to follow him and devote our lives to him.

God now reveals himself in a relational way through the person of the Holy Spirit. The Spirit dwells within us, and his presence is a transformative force in our lives. As we walk with him, he guides and directs us and keeps us from wandering. By speaking to us, encouraging us, enabling us, and empowering us, the Holy Spirit is walking intimately with us and speaking through us.

As we talk about God to others, our words should reflect a close, personal relationship with our Creator. It might be easier to present him to someone with a sales pitch, or reduce him to a set of morals and standards, but he chose to reveal himself differently to us—and thus our approach to others should be different as well. God intends for our relationship with him to be complex, dynamic, and personal—like our relationships with other people. As we engage in conversations with people around us, we should speak honestly about God—expressing our affection and wonder; confessing our frustration or confusion—with a familiarity that captures their attention and piques their curiosity.

People will be drawn to God not because we make claims for him that may seem too good to be true, and not because we have the moral high ground, but because they can't help but notice that we know something they don't. Or to put it more accurately, we know *someone* they don't.

THE LAW OF THE FARM

A farmer, perhaps more than most,
knows something about faith.

CHRISTINE HOOVER

RACHEL CAME TO NEW YORK to be a part of our training program. One thing we focus on is helping people turn up their spiritual volume. We want to see people make God more and more a part of their everyday language. Rachel already lived the Shema. She already breathed the Spirit throughout her day, and her language naturally focused on the work of the Father. Her love for him flowed out in her conversations, and she lived genuinely and unapologetically.

Rachel also really liked her nails to look good. She frequented the same nail salon, sitting with a different person each time. Each manicure provided quite a bit of time for conversation. And talking with Rachel naturally meant that someone in the salon was spiritually engaged.

As Rachel shared about her life and let her love for God enter into her speech, the workers were drawn to her. They all started looking forward to Rachel's visits so they could talk to her and ask her questions. They saw in her a unique picture of life and joy that they had not seen before. Pretty soon, Rachel knew everyone in the salon, including the male owner. He, too, was asking questions and was excited to engage in spiritual conversations.

One day, the owner did something that no business school would teach. Despite the financial ramifications, he presented Rachel with a proposition: If she were willing to come in once a week and lead a Bible study, he would close the salon an hour early so his workers could participate.

How does something like this happen? How does a business owner decide to close his shop early so that every one of his employees has the chance to learn more about Jesus—even before he himself is a follower of Jesus?

This wasn't a strategy that Rachel walked in with. It wasn't her vision to teach an entire salon of manicurists and nail technicians. She just went about her day, being herself and engaging people spiritually, and God found a way to use her to reach a whole bunch of people.

To return briefly to the farming analogy: Every time we use a Shema statement, it is like sowing a seed into the ground. The more seed we cast, the more likely it is that something will sprout and take root. When we learn to live comfortably in our spiritual skin and engage people in spiritual ways, it's like walking around with a pocket full of seed that is constantly falling around us. When we start to leave a trail of seed everywhere we go, we will start to see fruit in unexpected places—perhaps like a nail salon.

FRUITLESS FARMERS

Paul McCartney is one of the most successful songwriters of all time. He has written the most number one singles, contributed to the most number one albums on the US charts, won eighteen Grammys, and was even the first artist to broadcast live into space.[1] His work is said to have shaped the history of music. How does he do it? How has he written so many successful songs? He is talented, yes, but it's also about sheer volume. According to the Paul McCartney Project, he has written or collaborated on more than 730 songs.[2] In other words, he walks around, throwing out songs, casting them every which way, letting them land where they will—and some of them take root. The more songs, the more hits. The more seeds, the more growth. The more people we engage, the more people we reach.

That is the law of the farm.

It's so simple, and yet we have a way of complicating things. God asks us to cast seed and reap a harvest, but somewhere along the line we convince ourselves that first we need to study the proper way of casting seed. We then spend countless hours memorizing throwing techniques, debating which brand of seed is the best, and deciding which hour of the day we should cast that seed for maximum impact. We feel as if we know a lot about how to be a farmer, but we very rarely ever get around to actually farming. The sad thing is that God isn't interested in how well-versed we are in theories of seed casting; he wants us out in the field, casting seed and reaping a harvest. He's interested in our fruit.

This is why traditional gospel-presentation training has had so little impact. People leave the training knowing exactly what to say if they happen to find themselves in conversations conducive to sharing the gospel; but most people don't happen to find them-selves in conversations conducive to sharing the gospel. All that memorizing and theorizing only works under perfect conditions, which tends to mean we never use the techniques we've so proudly mastered. We've become farmers in theory and fruitless in reality. As Jim Elliff writes,

> We have the mistaken notion that evangelism is a
> choreographed set of ideas well laid out, perfectly
> transitioned, and flawlessly presented. Forget it. It's not
> this way. Many of us have tried this with frustration. It
> is much better to think of evangelism the way the Bible
> does—"sowing the seed" in any way you can. Any of us
> can do that.[3]

Let's compare two people. June follows Christ. She hasn't memorized a gospel presentation and doesn't know an impressive amount of theology, but she's in love with Jesus and wears that love for him on her sleeve. She lives out loud naturally, and God is a regular part of her language. Her overt spirituality often leads to people asking her questions about God or the Bible. When she doesn't know the answer, she tells them she isn't sure and would like to learn more.

Then there's Charles. He has taken evangelism courses, can clearly explain the points of the gospel in a logical way, and can answer most of the questions an unbeliever might ask him. But Charles doesn't bring God into his regular language. He isn't in the habit of letting his love for Jesus be known and seen through his interactions. In other words, he doesn't live out loud.

Which person do you think will have more spiritual fruit? In my experience, it's June. Every time! A person will have far more spiritual fruit by turning up their spiritual volume than by increasing their knowledge and skill.

Now, don't get me wrong, these things aren't mutually exclusive. The best scenario is when we are growing in spiritual volume, theological knowledge, and ministry skill. But if I'm putting these items on a scale of importance, spiritual volume wins out every time. Those who live out loud have far more fruitful gospel conversations than those who silently wait for the perfect conditions to employ their skills.

FAITHFUL FARMERS

I have always been struck by the parable of the talents. It is equally exciting and scary because it's about *faithfulness*. God has given me "talents" of truth to use and spread and talk about on his behalf. The more I use them—and use them well—the more he will give me.

> It will be like a man going on a journey, who called his servants and entrusted to them his property. To one he gave five talents, to another two, to another one, to each according to his ability. Then he went away. He who had received the five talents went at once and traded with them, and he made five talents more. So also he who had the two talents made two talents more. But he who had received the one talent went and dug in the ground and hid his master's money. Now after a long time the master of those servants came and settled accounts with them. And he who had received the five talents came forward, bringing five talents more, saying, "Master, you delivered

to me five talents; here, I have made five talents more."
His master said to him, "Well done, good and faithful
servant. You have been faithful over a little; I will set
you over much. Enter into the joy of your master." And
he also who had the two talents came forward, saying,
"Master, you delivered to me two talents; here, I have
made two talents more." His master said to him, "Well
done, good and faithful servant. You have been faithful
over a little; I will set you over much. Enter into the joy
of your master." He also who had received the one talent
came forward, saying, "Master, I knew you to be a hard
man, reaping where you did not sow, and gathering where
you scattered no seed, so I was afraid, and I went and hid
your talent in the ground. Here, you have what is yours."
But his master answered him, "You wicked and slothful
servant! You knew that I reap where I have not sown and
gather where I scattered no seed? Then you ought to have
invested my money with the bankers, and at my coming
I should have received what was my own with interest.
So take the talent from him and give it to him who has
the ten talents. For to everyone who has will more be
given, and he will have an abundance. But from the one
who has not, even what he has will be taken away. And
cast the worthless servant into the outer darkness. In that
place there will be weeping and gnashing of teeth."
MATTHEW 25:14-30

The exciting thing is that God doesn't spread out an equal
share of "talents" to everyone just for the sake of fairness. He gives
more to those who will do more with it, which means there is no

limit. I can grow in faithfulness and bear more and more fruit. The scary thing is also that God doesn't spread out an equal share of "talents" to everyone for the sake of fairness. If I'm not making good use of what he has given me, he will take it away. It's actually considered wicked if I have nothing to show for what God has entrusted to me.

He is like a master who is interested in increasing his wealth. He puts his resources in the hands of those who will use them best. He gives his seed to those who will cast it. He brings receptive people to those who will engage them. And those trustworthy servants will reap exponentially.

That is why being a servant of the living God is both scary and exciting. It's what turns nail salons into Bible studies and theoretical farmers into fruitful ones. A wasteland can become a burgeoning field when a few people with pockets full of seed decide to start casting it everywhere they go, expecting God to produce an abundant harvest. That is the law of the farm.

12

FOLLOW RECEPTIVITY

*Evangelism is not salesmanship! It is not urging
people, pressing them, coercing them, overwhelming
them, or subduing them. Evangelism is telling a
message. Evangelism is reporting good news.*

RICHARD HALVERSON

LET ME STOP AND CLARIFY for a moment. Living out loud is
not synonymous with living loudly. It is not a call to be obnoxious. Evangelism sometimes includes moments when we must set
aside our apprehensions and act outside of our comfort zones in
obedience to the Spirit's leading; but synthetically creating these
moments is not what I have in mind when I talk about living the
Shema. I'm not saying that we all need to become a little braver,
a little louder, and a little more forceful with our gospel presentations. I'm saying that a life lived out loud is one of natural, fre-
quent, authentic interactions that distinguish us as followers of
Jesus. In other words, it's about letting Shema statements become
our regular pattern of speech as we love God with all our heart,
mind, and strength.

This clarification is important because high-volume forceful-ness has left a bad taste in many mouths. So many Christians have given up on the idea of engaging people spiritually because they believe it means memorizing a scripted monologue, delivering it to people who aren't interested, and forcing them to listen. It's no wonder most of us squirm internally at the thought of it! That sort of interaction is not a true expression of evangelism.

I REALLY HAVE TO GO

In our training program, we send people out in groups of two to pray for strangers on the streets. We have been so encouraged by how many people are open to—and even desirous of—being prayed for. We have seen fruit from these times of intentionality, but we've also seen some people go into these moments with a somewhat skewed idea of the goal.

On one particular occasion, Kyle and Mike went out together to pray for people. When Mike approached a man and asked if he needed prayer for anything, the man responded with a standoffish, "I'm fine, thank you." Kyle interpreted that as the end of their interaction, but Mike interpreted it as a moment to press in. At first the man politely listened as Mike shared a presentation. When he responded that he wasn't interested, Mike pushed further and further. With every push, Kyle became less and less comfortable, and the man became later and later for work. As he kept insisting that he needed to go, Mike kept insisting that he needed Jesus. Kyle wanted to go hide under a rock, apologize for Mike, or step in and try to smooth out the awkward tension. Finally, in frustra-tion, the man just walked away.

Mike meant well, but even with the best of intentions we can't create receptivity where there isn't any. Mike felt that he needed to make something happen, but that wasn't Mike's job—it was God's. Unless God has prepared someone's heart, they will not be ready to respond to anything we say or do. People cannot be pressured into faith in Jesus. People cannot be forced to receive the good news of salvation through Christ alone. They have to feel like it's something good to receive. God is the only one who can bring them to that place. And for the guy on the street that day, God hadn't. And Mike couldn't.

Being bold and urgent about engaging people spiritually is biblical, and we can't shrink away from it. But it is important for us to recognize what God is doing in the moment. And we must recognize that spiritual engagement does not equate to forcefulness.

Most likely, at one time or another, we have all stood in Mike's shoes—or Kyle's, or even the guy on the street's. And that's not entirely bad. The point is not to put someone down for their zeal. In fact, in Philippians 1:15-18, we see Paul rejoicing over people who were preaching the gospel, even though some were doing so with bad motives.

PRESSING IN

We have a principle we use on our ministry team here in New York (a slogan, if you will): "Invest your time with those who are receptive, not with those who are not receptive." The idea is that we live out loud, sowing seed as we go about our day, and then we spend more time engaging with those people who are interested in talking about spiritual things.

Take Abdu, for example. He is from Somalia but lives in Harlem. (Or at least that's where he works selling bedsheets on the sidewalk.) I happen to walk down 125th Street several times a week, so one day I stopped and said hello. We began talking about his family, and I asked if everyone was in good health. He mentioned that his mother had a sickness, and I asked if I could pray for her. He said, "Yes, but not in the name of Jesus."

I could tell that Abdu wasn't very receptive to me, so I didn't offer to pray with him then and there. I did, however, pray for his mother on my own, and the next time I walked by, I told Abdu I had been praying for her. He was really surprised. First, because I remembered. Second, because no one really does that. I told him about how Isa ("Jesus" in Arabic) is a healer. Abdu seemed to shy away from the topic. I didn't push but told him it was great seeing him and that I would continue to pray.

The next time I saw Abdu, he asked me how I was doing, and I told him what God had been teaching me that day. The next time I passed by, I told Abdu about a Scripture I had been reading and he showed a little bit more interest. The following week, I asked Abdu if I could pray for God's favor on his business, and we prayed together right there in the middle of the sidewalk.

Weeks went by, and Abdu slowly became more and more receptive. I spoke openly as a spiritual person, but I never forced the conversation to go deeper than Abdu wanted it to go. After a while Abdu began asking questions. One day he asked if we could have dinner together. Soon he said he wanted to learn more about Jesus from the Injil (Gospels), and we began studying the Bible together.

Following receptivity is about knowing when to press in and when to be patient. In the beginning, I was spending maybe two or three minutes living out loud around Abdu. I wasn't pushing anything on him and was very respectful of his desires. Since he seemed unreceptive, I wasn't going to invest a lot of my time with him. As he became more receptive, I was open to giving him more of my time.

I know it could sound like I was being very stingy with my schedule. But when we become forceful and try to manufacture receptivity, it's almost as if we are exerting all our energy trying to pick crops before they are ready—tugging and tugging at immature veggies when a plethora of ripe ones are waiting in another part of the field.

When my son was young, he had that classic toy where you line up different shaped blocks with the corresponding holes. One day, he was holding a square block and trying to get it to go through the circle-shaped opening. No matter what he did, or how frustrated he became, it wasn't working. He was quite literally trying to shove a square peg through a round hole. After watching his wasted effort for a while, I showed him there was a square opening that would easily accommodate his block.

This reminds me of what Jesus teaches in Matthew 7:6: We shouldn't throw our pearls before swine. We shouldn't desperately, aggressively, anxiously beg people to respond to the gospel as we try to push them where they don't want to go. Instead, we should have conversations that reveal our love for God and let him worry about making things fit.

GAUGING RECEPTIVITY

I often get asked how to know if you're being too forceful with people. How can we avoid being pushy without missing opportunities? After many years of leading a ministry that emphasizes spiritual engagement, I can tell you that there are a few common ways that people tend to react to Shema statements. Some will agree with them. Some will disagree with them. Some will ignore them. Some will ask you what you mean by them. Let their response inform where you take the conversation.

If you congratulate someone on the birth of their baby by saying that God has blessed them, and they respond by saying that God had nothing to do with it—move on. You are just being who you are, and so are they, and that's okay. If you say something spiritual and the other person acts like you didn't say anything, that's okay too. Don't worry about it. Be authentically who you are and don't demand that they respond in any particular way. Just keep casting the seed as you go along.

From my experience, I can assure you that there will be many times when saying something spiritual will bring up a question or draw out the spirituality in someone else. Continuing to engage at such times isn't forcing the issue; it's responding to momentum. But make sure you're not talking *at* the other person. Talk *with* them. You're not *selling*, you're *conversing*. Share stories, answer questions, ask some questions of your own. As long as the other person engages in the conversation with you, there is no need for spiritual timidity or spiritual forcefulness.

Honestly, these are just basic principles for how to talk to people in general. For some reason, Christians tend to think of spiritual things as a whole new category of communication. We can tell when people are enjoying stories about our kids or when they're interested in the same sports we are. We know when we've reached common ground on just about any other topic, but tell us to bring up spiritual things and suddenly we lose our conversation skills.

As followers of Jesus and lovers of God, we are spiritual people who naturally like to talk about spiritual things. We reflect our love for God by using Shema statements. Because we're following Jesus, we bring him up in conversation. Nothing about that has to be weird. We don't need to force anything, and we don't need to freeze. If God uses our overt spirituality to draw someone to himself, then our engaging someone in conversation will not be about trapping the person into listening to a monologue about Jesus; it will be about having a dialogue about things in life that matter.

So the short and simple answer for how to gauge receptivity is this: If someone opens the door in conversation, walk through it. If they slam it shut, don't try to kick it down.

My friend Noy goes to the college campus near his home and strikes up conversations with students. If a student seems interested and willing to talk more, Noy will get a phone number and follow up with a text. Sometimes his text leads to more fruitful conversations with that person.

Noy has been doing this for several years. In the course of talking to students and following their receptivity, he began to notice something interesting: Many students who were once unreceptive are becoming more receptive. The other day he was having a conversation with a student who was very interested in meeting and talking more. When Noy went to put the student's contact information into his phone, he found he already had it. Two years earlier, they had exchanged numbers after a good conversation, but at the time, the student wasn't ready to go deeper and never responded to Noy's follow-up text. Neither one remembered the earlier contact. Variations of this story have become increasingly common for Noy, and he has come to realize that no conversation is wasted by God—not even ones that end with an ignored text. Our job is to cast the seed. God brings the increase.

Noy doesn't need to aggressively send a thousand follow-up texts in an effort to force receptivity. Only God can develop a person's receptivity, and Noy just has to wait for it. As he lives out his spirituality on that campus, he is open and available for God to use him. He engages people to see who is receptive and goes deeper when he finds those who are.

Evangelism can be a forced confrontation or it can unfold organically and naturally as we follow people's receptivity. When someone is receptive to who we are as followers of Jesus, we press in. When they aren't, we don't. When they really have to go—to work, to school, to get away from us—we let them. But when we see God moving, we join him. Square pegs in search of a square hole.

13

THE DOORWAY OF BROKENNESS

All of our infirmities, whatever they are, are just opportunities for God to display his gracious work in us.

CHARLES SPURGEON

MY FRIEND JACOB is a great guy. He loves Jesus and wants to use every talent and resource he has to see people fall in love with God. But Jacob also struggles sometimes to engage people spiritually. He recently shared with me one of those struggles, and if you're anything like Jacob and me, I'm sure you'll relate:

It was just a normal day. My wife and I were running some errands with our two kids. We needed some crafting supplies (because our kids were toddlers and that's how you survive those years) so we ended up at Michael's craft store. As my wife was hunting down finger paints and smelly markers, I was killing time in an aisle filled with stuff for decorating cakes.

I was comparing frosting tips when I happened to notice a woman across the store from me. She was in a wheelchair, and it was obvious she had recently suffered some sort of ailment that kept her from walking.

Immediately (and almost audibly) God told me to go pray for her to be healed. As quickly as God told me to do it, I started making excuses.

"I actually was thinking about baking a cake and really need to decide what supplies to get. Besides, my wife probably needs my help with the kids. . . . I think I hear them now."

God wouldn't relent, so he and I went back and forth for a while. I knew what he wanted me to do, and I even knew that I was skirting it because of disbelief. Yes, I was scared to go up to a total stranger. Yes, I wasn't sure how she would respond to being prayed for in a craft supply store. But more than those things, I was really worried that I would pray for healing and God wouldn't heal her. I was worried that he was setting me (and, worse, himself) up to fail. So even though I knew what God wanted me to do, and even though I felt compassion for the woman, I disobeyed. I left the store with finger paints and smelly markers and a heavy heart.

My kids aren't toddlers anymore. That was quite a few years ago, but I still remember what that woman looked like. I still remember God inviting me into a moment of bravery and spiritual engagement and maybe even supernatural healing. And I remember what it felt like to turn him down and walk away without enough faith to do it. It haunts me. I know he is gracious, and he knows that I'm sorry. He still gives me opportunities to engage people, and I am increasingly becoming trustworthy with those opportunities. But that moment in Michael's is one moment I won't get back. I will never know exactly what that woman and I could have experienced that day.

I still wonder what happened to her. I wonder whether God prompted someone else to pray for her, and they obeyed, and she got healed, and he got glorified, and I missed out. I hope so. It would be pretty cool to hear the other side of that story one day in heaven.

I think Jacob's experience is pretty common. Truth be told, I think many Christians don't even go so far as to wrestle with God in that moment. Many don't recognize it as an open door. To them, brokenness is merely a reality, not an opportunity. But Scripture shows us that God uses circumstances of brokenness to prepare people to receive him. Those who are weary are invited to come to him.[1] Those who are displaced are seeking him.[2] Those who need healing call out to him.[3] God often tills the soil of a person's heart through brokenness. Where there is brokenness, it is safe to assume God is giving us an opportunity. And if you've noticed, brokenness happens to be pretty much everywhere.

This world, and everyone in it, experiences the consequences of the Fall. Because of the Fall there is death, disease, and suffering. No one is immune to brokenness. You can talk to any person from anyplace in the world, and if you explore even a little about their life or family, you will hear stories of sickness and struggle, setbacks and suffering, hardship and pain. People are hurting and tired. They're looking for some relief.

This sad reality, which touches us all, also means that you and

I are surrounded by opportunity. People are looking for physical, emotional, and spiritual healing, and we know the God who gives it. The Fall has given us unlimited opportunities for spiritual engagement and ministry.

My friends Hojatt and Sehar have been coming over for dinner lately. They aren't believers, but because they have been in our home, they have heard many Shema statements. We pray for our dinner when they are with us because we pray for our dinner when they aren't with us. We talk around the table about our days, and that usually includes some story about spiritual interactions. Even when we're playing board games, it's pretty normal for someone to blurt out something like, "I know God wants me to consider others as more important than myself, but I'm definitely out to win this one."

All that to say, Hojatt and Sehar are pretty used to hearing Shema statements by now. Sometimes they ask questions, and sometimes they don't. Sometimes those questions lead to a discussion, and we open the Bible and look at something together and talk about it for a while. Other times they don't, and that's okay.

One night Hojatt was repeatedly gasping for air. He had what seemed like terrible hiccups, and he was perpetually holding his throat. I asked him if he was okay, and he shared that he was getting nervous because for the last three to four months his throat had been hurting. Sometimes it was so bad he wasn't able to swallow.

Toward the end of the night, I asked Hojatt if I could pray for him in the name of Jesus that his throat would be healed. This wasn't the typical Shema statement he was accustomed to. Even though it was a little strange for him, he said yes. I asked permission to put my hand on his throat, and I prayed in the name of Jesus that God the Father would heal Hojatt. The next time I saw him, I asked him how his throat was. He sort of nonchalantly said it had stopped hurting right around the time we prayed.

This isn't a story of Hojatt suddenly falling to his knees and acknowledging God as a healer. In fact, it's probably a bit more like the story where ten lepers were healed and only one came back to thank Jesus for it. Hojatt is currently one of the nine. The point is that opportunities like this are everywhere. They won't always be spectacularly supernatural, but they will be a chance for God to meet someone in their brokenness. And sometimes, that prayer for healing will stand out in a way that a hundred other Shema statements don't.

Jesus' earthly ministry was one of healing. It was often by addressing struggles with brokenness that he engaged people spiritually. Matthew 4:23-25 gives us a glimpse of this:

> He went throughout all Galilee, teaching in their
> synagogues and proclaiming the gospel of the kingdom
> and healing every disease and every affliction among
> the people. So his fame spread throughout all Syria,
> and they brought him all the sick, those afflicted with
> various diseases and pains, those oppressed by demons,
> those having seizures, and paralytics, and he healed
> them. And great crowds followed him from Galilee and
> the Decapolis, and from Jerusalem and Judea, and from
> beyond the Jordan.

It isn't at all surprising that when Jesus sent out the seventy-two, he told them, "Whenever you enter a town and they receive you, eat what is set before you. Heal the sick in it and say to them, 'The kingdom of God has come near to you.'"[4] The effects of the

Fall were so pervasive that, in pretty much any household they entered, there would be people there who needed healing. Jesus knew that deliverance from suffering was such a powerful doorway to spiritual receptivity that he specifically instructed those being sent out to include it as part of their spiritual-engagement plan.

I follow this same model whenever I engage people spiritually. I often ask, "How is your family?" "Is there any sickness in your home?" "How is your health?" Many people try to create a ramp to spiritual dialogue when a ramp is already sitting right in front of them. Many people who are not ready to talk about spiritual things are nonetheless searching for healing. People are physically and emotionally suffering, and Jesus is the answer. Offering to pray for people is one of the most profound ways I have seen to meet them in their hurting.

DON'T OPEN THE DOOR

There are a few reasons why you might be hesitant to pray for healing. Maybe, like Jacob, you're a bit worried that God won't do it. What if you seek out brokenness and use it as a door to spiritual conversation and then God leaves everyone hanging?

Wouldn't that be worse than just leaving the door shut?

The answer, I think, is twofold. Brokenness is an opportunity for God to display his power. When he miraculously heals, it can jump-start a person's heart and invigorate their faith. But even when God chooses not to heal, brokenness is an opportunity for us to display love. Caring enough to ask questions and pray for someone is not common in our society.

When people encounter this kind of love, it can capture their attention and draw them toward God. Either way, we needn't get caught up in worrying about the outcome. God is in charge of what prayer produces, both in physical healing and in spiritual awakening.

Another reason some people are hesitant to pray for healing is because they are distracted by theological positions. Maybe you're not really a "gift of healing" type of person. That's all right because I'm not even talking about the gift of healing. The truth is, we all pray, no matter how charismatic or noncharismatic we might be. We ask God to heal people when they're sick. We plead with him to fix brokenness in our lives. We look to him to restore what has been splintered. Living out loud simply brings that habit into our everyday conversations.

Because people are broken physically, emotionally, and spiritually; and because God heals; and because we love others; and because we believe in prayer—we have countless opportunities for spiritual engagement. Whether it's with a stranger in a craft store or a friend sitting at our dinner table, God is inviting us to be a part of what he is doing. It's a door worth opening.

14

CAVING IN TO CULTURE

The world is waiting to hear an authentic voice,
a voice from God—not an echo of what others
are doing and saying, but an authentic voice.

A. W. TOZER

WE LIVE IN an increasingly post-Christian society. Our culture is shifting quickly, and the common thinking no longer reflects a biblical worldview. Where principles of morality were once pretty unanimous, they are now up for grabs. So what does it look like for followers of Jesus to live in such a cultural moment? How do we not lose ourselves in the midst of the ebbing trends? After all, like most North American Christians, we've lived our entire lives as a part of Western culture. How can we even tell where our thinking has become more cultural than biblical?

This may seem like a very modern problem, but the need to combat the influences of culture is nothing new. Paul saw the same issues in the churches of his day, and he offers a solution:

Do not be conformed to this world, but be transformed
by the renewal of your mind, that by testing you may
discern what is the will of God, what is good and
acceptable and perfect.

ROMANS 12:2

We are new creations in Christ, living out new identities that
have the power to shape our surroundings. When we look around
and notice that we have lost a bit of our potency, there's a good
chance it started with conforming to the culture. Every day, the
influences around us apply continual pressure and shape who we
are . . . unless we actively resist.

Paul's method of resisting? Instead of being conformed, be
transformed. Renew your mind. Every day. Again and again. Go
back to what you know is true and dwell on it. Remind yourself
of who you are and live into it. Let God completely renovate your
mind until you start to look and think and speak like the person
you truly are in Christ. Continually renewing our minds is how we
battle the conforming pressures of the world. It's how we think like
citizens of heaven rather than like citizens of this world.

So what does cultural influence have to do with our ability to
engage people spiritually? A lot! One of the most prominent ways
that our culture influences us is by rendering us spiritually silent.
Our culture has told us to stop talking—that we have nothing
worthwhile to say—and we have largely acquiesced. But it's not as
if culture walked up to us one day and told us to keep our mouths
shut and we kindly obliged. Laying the groundwork for our current situation was far more subtle than that.

Take naturalism, for example. Naturalism is the belief that
there is no God or spiritual reality and that the laws of nature are

behind the daily causes and effects of life. You and I know the Bible says otherwise. The Bible speaks of a God who is actively involved in the affairs of humanity. We may know the correct answer. We may say we ascribe to a biblical worldview, but functionally many of us think and live as naturalists. We go about our days not giving much thought to spiritual things. We don't really see a spiritual connection to the car accident, the autoimmune disorder, or the finance report due at work.

Imagine this scenario with me: You enter a crowded bus. You find a seat near the back and slide in toward the window. At the next stop, a man boards the bus and grabs the last remaining seat next to you.

Now imagine that someone else walks up and asks both of you why you are sitting where you are. What would your answer be? Perhaps something like this: "Well, we are both headed somewhere on the same bus and happened to get the last two seats. That's why we're here."

From a naturalistic perspective, your answer would be true. Everything just happened the way it did. But would it even cross your mind to reply that you were both sitting there because God orchestrated it? Would you ever find yourself thinking, *God wants me to sit next to this man for the next seven stops*? How would your interaction with your seatmate change if you saw it not as happenstance, but as spiritually significant? I'm willing to bet you would be more likely to look up from your phone or take off your headphones, strike up a conversation, and see where things go.

As Christians, we have (mostly unwittingly) conformed ourselves to the naturalistic worldview around us, and this has effectively silenced us. We don't *think* about spiritual realities throughout the day, so we don't *talk* about spiritual realities throughout the day. Our language flows out of our (actual) worldview.

Another way culture has influenced us is through evangelistic baggage. Evangelistic Christians are often stereotyped as rude, judgmental, out-of-touch, corner-yelling bigots. Our culture has a negative view of evangelism, and that view has rubbed off on many Christians as well. We don't want to be associated with the kinds of interactions that our culture openly mocks. Some have written sermons, books, and articles about how not to look like those out-of-touch corner evangelists.

The thing is, our aversion to certain forms of evangelism isn't biblical; it's cultural. While we go to great lengths to differentiate ourselves from the stereotypes, some of those methods look very similar to the forms of evangelism we find in Scripture.

Maybe that makes you cringe. I get it. I too have felt uncomfortable and even embarrassed about being associated with certain evangelists. I'm not trying to defend any particular style, but I do want to make one thing very clear: *Any* form of evangelism is more honoring to God than no evangelism at all; and *every* form of evangelism is more effective at times than no evangelism. As D. L. Moody reportedly said to someone who was criticizing his methods, "I like my way of sharing the gospel better than your way of not sharing it."[1]

When I walk down the sidewalk and encounter a street corner evangelist, I feel a tinge of discomfort. And though that style doesn't mesh well with my own approach, I thank God for that person who cared enough to put himself out there. Some people need to hear from a John-the-Baptist-type evangelist, even if it makes other people uncomfortable. Even if it makes *me* uncomfortable. And even if John the Baptist would likely be satirized in a skit on *Saturday Night Live* if he were still around today.

God ordained that people will be drawn to him through

hearing—that is, through words; and that should make us much more uncomfortable with our silence than we are with various forms of evangelism we happen to dislike. If we are more influenced by cultural opinion than by Scripture, we will emphasize trendy over truthful, and it will lead to very little fruit. The point is that this cultural baggage has influenced our thinking, and the effect, once again, is silence.

SOCIAL PRESSURES

Peer pressure, or social pressure, is probably the most powerful form of cultural influence we face. A team led by neuroscientist Gregory Berns conducted a study on social conformity. They wanted to know whether people would deliberately answer a question incorrectly just to fit in. What they found is that the human brain responds in one of two ways to social pressure. When we feel pressured to answer a question incorrectly and we decide to cave to that pressure, our brain literally adjusts our perception to believe the wrong answer. When we decide to answer correctly and push back on social pressure, our brain responds with emotional pain. So we either alter our thinking to conform to social pressure or experience the unpleasant emotional load of nonconformity.[2]

Why does it matter? Because our predisposition is to give in to the social pressures around us. Our brain wants us to. The ones doing the pressuring want us to. And when we do give in, it shifts our thinking to conform to those pressures even more.

Feel like you're swimming upstream? You're not alone. It doesn't have to be overwhelming, but it's going to take some awareness on your part because so many of the social pressures that are built into everyday life go completely unnoticed. I mean, you know you feel pressured, but you're not always sure why, or where it's coming from, or how it's influencing you. So let's take a look at some of the most common ways we experience social pressures. And then let's deconstruct them a bit.

1. Acceptance

We want to be accepted, and we feel pressure to do things that will make us acceptable. This is the fear of man the Bible speaks of.[3] We want people to like us, and we fear they won't if we engage them spiritually. So, rather than live into the new identity Christ has given us, we create for ourselves an idol of acceptance and conform to what we think our culture wants.

The irony of pursuing acceptance is that most of the pressure we feel is a mirage. Assuming that people will reject us, we avoid spiritual conversations. But, in most cases, they actually will accept us for the spiritual people we are. If you're a good neighbor who treats people with kindness, if you're a contributing and hard-working member of the workplace, if you serve and love those around you, most people will respect and appreciate your living an authentically spiritual life.

2. Appropriateness

We want people to feel as though we are talking about the right things, at the right times, in the right places. This is the pressure we feel to keep conversations about God and spirituality in the realm of church or our believing community. We feel it's better to hide our spirituality than to display it "inappropriately." We shy away from talking to coworkers, for instance, because it might be deemed inappropriate to bring up spiritual things at work.

In large part, we have misinterpreted the pressure and created an unnecessary boundary. The real cultural pressure (which isn't a bad one) is to honor people and show them respect in their religious beliefs. If people are afraid they will get a lecture whenever you come around, then your conversation about God and spiritual things is inappropriate. If you aren't getting your work done because you're too busy badgering people about coming to church, you're being inappropriate. If you're speaking against what others believe, your conversations are inappropriate. But if you honor and respect people and what they believe, most will find it completely acceptable for you to live out a genuine expression of your spirituality wherever you are.

3. Family

We all have roles to play in our families. Parent, child, spouse, sibling, cousin—each one comes with pressure to conform to a powerful family dynamic. Have you ever noticed that whenever you're with your family, you immediately revert to the same way of relating to everyone as you did when you were fifteen? We all grow up filling certain roles in our families, and those dynamics don't change easily. If you're the only Christian in your family, the pressure can be magnified. It can feel like hypocrisy, disrespect, or rebellion to display your spirituality to your family members, and the thought of becoming the black sheep can cause you to avoid spiritual conversations.

The truth is that most of our families love us for who we are. They might not want to get into "talking religion" at the dinner table, but they want to know the real you. Living out loud is a natural way to be authentically yourself, and most of the time those who love you will be glad you are being real. It's okay if you're struggling in your walk with Jesus and they see some hypocrisy in your life. Talk about it. Even our failures as believers can become powerful Shema statements to members of our families and others.

4. Scarce harvest

Now more than ever before, we are bombarded with cultural influences. We carry them around in our pocket-sized phones. We welcome culture into our living rooms and bedrooms and family rooms and anywhere else a screen will fit. We soak it up in the news, and we can't escape it in the grocery store tabloid headlines. And with all these messages vying for our attention, it's easy to assume that everyone around us must think and act like the media portrays.

As Christians, we're told that nobody wants to hear about Jesus. We're sold the lie that the landscape is barren and there is no hope for a harvest. We feel pressured to give up and stop bothering people with our spirituality. The truth is, however, that we are surrounded by people waiting to be engaged with spiritual things. Christians are not the only people experiencing the pressure of a naturalistic culture. Many unbelieving people feel pressured to suppress thoughts and questions about spiritual things. This doesn't mean they're disinterested. In fact, encountering someone who confidently lives out their authentic spirituality might become a catalyst for them to push back on that pressure.

In all these instances, the majority of the social pressure we feel is self-induced. People don't harbor all the negative feelings about spirituality we think they do. Though there are always a few hard cases out there, we project their negativity onto the many and feel as if the pressure is pervasive. It's not! Let's not misinterpret whatever resistance we might feel. When we spend more time engaging individuals than we do ingesting the culture, we will find that many of these daunting cultural pressures have no bearing on our relationships.

That's why it's important for me to emphasize that living out loud is about engaging individuals, not taking on the entire culture. It's about being a refreshing countercultural presence in one relationship and one conversation at a time. God isn't calling us to a showdown with our culture. He's inviting us to love individual people—the people we see and interact with every day. He's providing us with opportunities to engage the woman who lives next door, the mail carrier, a coworker, or the pizza delivery guy. People with faces and names. Real-life people. John Piper put it this way:

> It is a mistake to look at the "culture" and assume that all the unbelieving people are in lockstep with the spirit of the age. In fact, someone's child just died. Someone just found out he has cancer. Someone just lost his job at 55. Someone just had a terrifying dream about hell. Someone alone in a hotel room just happened to read the story of the prodigal son. Someone has just decided his life of self-indulgence is meaningless. Some young couple has just had a long conversation about the absence of moral standards to pass on to their children. Someone just felt a wave of guilt pass over his soul, and a deep sense that he is accountable to a Creator.
>
> In other words, we make a huge mistake if we forget that people get saved one at a time as unique individuals, not as mere specimens of the "culture." At any given

moment in the secularization of our culture, God is at work in ten thousand ways to prepare particular individuals to hear the gospel.[4]

Living out loud is about letting the things of your heart flow out of your mouth. Sometimes it means you need to take a good look at what happens to be in your heart. What patterns of thinking have infiltrated your identity? What assumptions have suppressed your spirituality? What pressures have silenced your speech? We live in a world that wants our conformity, yet we are called to seek transformation instead.

Allow God to remind you again and again of the truth about who you are. Remember that you are a new creation, called to a new life that is displayed in new ways of speaking. Ask God to show you how you might be caving in to culture—what influences you, what pressures you—and ask him to renew your mind. Then go out into the culture as a transformed person and engage people who need transformation. You never know which countercultural Shema statement might be the one that changes everything.

15

THE EVILS OF FRIENDSHIP EVANGELISM

Ah, you have never truly found Jesus if
you do not tell others about Him!

CHARLES SPURGEON

AS BELIEVERS, WE KNOW THAT the good news of the gospel is both spoken and displayed. We know that people sometimes become interested in Jesus by seeing the way we live as his followers. We know we are called to love people, no matter how spiritually receptive they may seem. With these things in mind, many Christians have turned to friendship evangelism as a method for engaging people spiritually. They have worked hard to build relationships with unbelievers, hoping and praying those relationships will one day open the door for them to share the gospel. "I'm showing the gospel with my actions right now, but someday I will share it with my words," they tell themselves. That is what friendship evangelism is all about, and they have been told that it's an authentic and refreshing approach to sharing Jesus with people.

With such good motives and such overwhelming support for friendship evangelism, how could I possibly say that it's bad? To stand against friendship evangelism must mean that I am anti-friendship and see people as projects. This, however, could not be further from the truth.

I believe the display of the gospel in the context of relationships is incredibly important. I believe we should get to know unbelievers and they should know us, and we should be ready to give an answer for the hope we have. Unbelievers should have Christian friends who are there for them when they lose their jobs, or get cancer, or can't shake their depression.

But I also believe that hiding our spirituality in the name of developing those friendships is wrong. This is where I take issue with the idea of friendship evangelism. I don't support the unbiblical ideas that undergird it. And I don't buy into the false beliefs that people must accept in order to support it.

I'm also concerned that, time and time again, it never produces spiritual engagement. When we pull back the curtain, I believe friendship evangelism does more to hinder the advancement of the gospel than promote it.

THE OLD BAIT AND SWITCH

If there is one thing we've learned from the world of romantic comedies, it's that you should never start a relationship by actively hiding some large part of who you are. It's never long before the other person finds out you have a child you forgot to mention, or you aren't actually the person you said you were, or you don't have the job you said you did. These tropes are popular because they create an absurd sort of tension that drives the comedic aspects of the romantic storyline. We all feel the escalating peril as the lies and coverups and near misses pile up, one on top of the other, until the dam breaks.

Typically, these characters have convinced themselves that falling in love will create a foundation that can withstand the weight of eventually exposing the truth. They build a relationship while postponing the inevitable reveal. We watch as (over and over again) they look for the "right moment" to bring it up, and we cringe because we know they are going about it all wrong.

Though we know this approach is rife with pitfalls, so many Christians have adopted it when it comes to spiritually engaging the people around them. Friendship evangelism says that we must first spend a significant amount of time getting to know someone, developing a friendship, building trust, and earning a voice. Once we feel that we have earned the right to speak to them about spiritual things, we start bringing it up in conversation. Friendship evangelism is attractive because it allows us to gain momentum in a relationship without the spiritual elements we assume will create friction. But there are several things glaringly wrong with this approach:

1. It ignores the fact that, all throughout Scripture, we are called to talk about God all the time. Whether we're living out the Shema, the Great Commission, or the simple admonition to "rejoice always,"[1] it should be impossible for us not to talk about God with those around us.

2. It assumes that talking about spiritual things will create friction. Most people are willing to engage in authentic spiritual conversations. Most people are willing to be

friends with spiritual people, even if they themselves aren't interested in spiritual things. So, in reality, being obvious about our identity doesn't usually create the friction we fear.

3. It undermines the trust that friendships are built on. Hiding a large part of who you are with the intention to expose it later doesn't make you a trustworthy voice in someone's life. You are trying to "earn the right to speak," but what you are actually doing is sabotaging your credibility and integrity. It's the old bait and switch: Hide who you really are until you hook someone into a friendship, and then show your true colors. People will hate the fact that you are inauthentic more than the fact that you are spiritual.

4. It creates an impossible expectation to find the "right moment." If you aren't obviously spiritual from conversation number one, it's twice as hard to bring up spiritual things in conversation number two. Conversation number three is three times as hard. By the fourth conversation, the situation feels too far gone. It's like asking someone their name after you've had a handful of conversations with them. There isn't a "right moment" because the friendship has gone too far to make introductions again. Finding the "right moment" can be so stressful for people that they either actively avoid it or turn it into a dramatic conversation that feels more like a confession than anything else. The best way to avoid all that anxiety and confusion is to be who you are from the get-go.

5. It's really hard to pull off unless Jesus isn't all that central to your identity. It's one thing to hide something you've done. It's something else entirely to hide who you really are. If you

can be friends with someone for a good long time without even accidentally blurting out spiritual things, then you might want to evaluate the real place of Jesus in your life. If you wait to bring up spiritual things until the friendship is well established, the other person's natural reaction will be to ask, "How could this be such a big part of your life, and yet I never knew about it?" And the only true response to that question is, "I guess it really isn't such a big part of my life."

6. It reduces spiritual engagement to a method for sharing the gospel rather than a way of life. Remember, living out loud is not a new, alternative way to evangelize. It is learning to live out your true identity as a new creation in Christ. It's about *who you are*, not something you *do*. Friendship evangelism keeps the focus on our *approach* rather than our *identity*. Living out loud means simply being obvious about who you are and letting God do the work of moving hearts toward him as people interact with you.

7. It isn't loving. Friendships happen when people turn to each other in their need, in their confusion, in their celebration, in dreaming and asking and giving. It is incredibly unloving to consciously leave God out of all those moments. Can you really give your friends advice that isn't based on what you know as truth? Can you rejoice with them without pointing to Jesus as the source of all good things? Can you forgive them and seek their forgiveness without referencing the ultimate Forgiver? To say you're a follower of Jesus and yet have friendships devoid of any mention of Jesus isn't loving; it's disingenuous.

Not to beat a dead horse, but friendship evangelism is harmful. I don't say that lightly. It is clearly unbiblical, ineffective, and has single-handedly silenced many well-intentioned believers. In Luke 11:33, Jesus himself says, "No one after lighting a lamp puts it in a cellar or under a basket, but on a stand, so that those who enter may see the light." Friendship evangelism says, "Go ahead and hide your light for a while. You can pull it out at just the right moment." Any strategy that asks us to hide who we are as followers of Jesus is not worth embracing.

On top of that, we shouldn't walk into conversations assuming our spirituality isn't welcome. At the height of the COVID-19 pandemic, I was having a conversation with some acquaintances, including a woman I had just met. Our world was facing a serious health crisis, people were scared, and tensions were growing; so naturally, these were the types of shoot-the-breeze topics you covered with people you barely knew. We were talking about how people were responding to the cultural moment when the woman offered her thoughts.

"Everyone just needs to take a deep breath, have some CBD, and center themselves."

In one brief statement, she told me a lot about who she was. I knew where she looked for hope and peace and how she responded to stress. I knew something about how she viewed the world and where she turned for answers. And the thing is, it wasn't weird. The conversation moved right along without skipping a beat. She wasn't awkward or pushy or apologetic. She had no agenda, and she didn't even realize what she was doing because she was just being who she was.

We Christians have spent far too much time suppressing our spirituality when it is actually really easy to be our genuine spiritual selves in conversations. No one else is walking around asking permission to be themselves. People aren't put off by genuine expressions of spirituality. We can let our love for God flow out into our language, and more often than not, the conversation will move right along without skipping a beat.

My friend Shelby loves India and talks about it often. My friend Josh tells a lot of stories that include his road biking adventures. My friend Anya has a toddler and loves to share every new milestone. My friend Peter is remodeling his house and always has an update on the progress. I know things my friends care about because they tell me about them. I don't have a proclivity for India. I don't ride a bike or have a toddler or love home renovations; but I have never once resented my friends for being authentic and giving me a window into their lives. And you know what? If I ever need to find some good tikka masala, I know who to ask.

This is what living out loud looks like. It's about living out our identity as followers of Jesus obviously, in every context, unapologetically, and with authenticity. It's not a method, but an essence. And because it is not something we do, but the way that we are, it isn't something we can turn on and off according to circumstance.

SUSAN'S STORY

Susan had been getting together with her neighbor Abeer for a while. They had kids the same age, and they would go to each other's homes for playdates. Abeer was a Bangladeshi Muslim, and Susan really wanted to share the gospel with her, but she had no idea how to bring it up.

They had been together many times, and Susan had never mentioned spiritual things. How could she do it now without it being completely awkward? Every time they got together, Susan would agonize a bit more.

Susan was part of one of our house churches here in New York City. Every week she talked about her desire to share with Abeer. Every week her house church rallied around her and prayed for her to have the courage and opportunity to spiritually engage Abeer. And every week Susan would come back confessing that she still hadn't done it. This went on for months.

One day, as usual, Susan called Abeer and asked if she wanted to come over and play. Abeer, as usual, said she would love to. But then something very unusual happened. When Abeer showed up at Susan's house, she was alone. Susan opened the door and (noticing the lack of kids) gave a confused look. Abeer announced, "I am ready to pray." Susan realized that Abeer had misheard her invitation to "play" and instead came over ready and excited to pray.

I have thought about this story a lot, and I think there are at least two ways to understand what happened. I think both ways are true. On the one hand, God knew that Susan wanted to engage Abeer, and he knew she was struggling to do it, so he graciously brought it up for her. He orchestrated a verbal misunderstanding to open up their friendship to spiritual conversations.

On the other hand, during all that time when Susan was agonizing over how to bring up spiritual things with Abeer, all she had to do was ask one simple question: "Do you want to pray?" And Abeer was ready! Susan didn't need to worry about how to say it, or how Abeer would receive it, or if it was the right moment, or if she had earned the right to speak yet. Their friendship was open to spiritual conversations all along, and Susan didn't realize it.

Engaging people spiritually doesn't have to create a storm of anxiety in our minds. Suppressing our spirituality is a tactic of the enemy, not a call from God. This means that engaging people spiritually is a whole lot easier than you may realize. If you love God, and you enjoy talking about what you love, just be yourself around your friends and God will use you to draw them to himself.

Perhaps as you are reading this you have already begun building relationships in the name of friendship evangelism. Maybe you feel discouraged and wonder where to go from here. One of the best ways to live out loud is to talk to people about what God is teaching you. Start there. Talk to your friends about your new conviction to be open and obvious about your love for God. If you have been looking for the right moment, it's now.

DON'T TAKE MY WORD FOR IT

This isn't a conclusion I came to on my own. Here are a few of the passages that led me to reject friendship evangelism. I invite you to allow Scripture to influence your thinking:

> It shall be to you as a sign on your hand and as a memorial between your eyes, that the law of the LORD may be in your mouth. For with a strong hand the LORD has brought you out of Egypt.
> EXODUS 13:9

> I will bless the LORD at all times; his praise shall continually be in my mouth. My soul makes its boast in the LORD; let the humble hear and be glad. Oh, magnify the LORD with me, and let us exalt his name together!
> PSALM 34:1-3

Then my tongue shall tell of your righteousness and of your praise all the day long.
PSALM 35:28

He put a new song in my mouth, a song of praise to our God. Many will see and fear, and put their trust in the LORD.
PSALM 40:3

In God we have boasted continually, and we will give thanks to your name forever.
PSALM 44:8

My soul will be satisfied as with fat and rich food, and my mouth will praise you with joyful lips.
PSALM 63:5

Come and hear, all you who fear God, and I will tell what he has done for my soul.
PSALM 66:16

My mouth is filled with your praise, and with your glory all the day.
PSALM 71:8

My mouth will tell of your righteous acts, of your deeds of salvation all the day, for their number is past my knowledge.
PSALM 71:15

For me it is good to be near God; I have made the Lord
GOD my refuge, that I may tell of all your works.

PSALM 73:28

We give thanks to you, O God; we give thanks, for your
name is near. We recount your wondrous deeds.

PSALM 75:1

I will sing of the steadfast love of the LORD, forever; with
my mouth I will make known your faithfulness to all
generations.

PSALM 89:1

Blessed are the people who know the festal shout, who
walk, O LORD, in the light of your face, who exult in
your name all the day and in your righteousness are
exalted.

PSALM 89:15-16

Oh give thanks to the LORD; call upon his name; make
known his deeds among the peoples!

PSALM 105:1

Let the redeemed of the LORD say so, whom he has
redeemed from trouble and gathered in from the lands,
from the east and from the west, from the north and
from the south.

PSALM 107:2-3

One generation shall commend your works to another, and shall declare your mighty acts. On the glorious splendor of your majesty, and on your wondrous works, I will meditate. They shall speak of the might of your awesome deeds, and I will declare your greatness. They shall pour forth the fame of your abundant goodness and shall sing aloud of your righteousness.

PSALM 145:4-7

And you will say in that day: "Give thanks to the LORD, call upon his name, make known his deeds among the peoples, proclaim that his name is exalted."

ISAIAH 12:4

And proclaim as you go, saying, "The kingdom of heaven is at hand."

MATTHEW 10:7

So everyone who acknowledges me before men, I also will acknowledge before my Father who is in heaven.

MATTHEW 10:32

And he said to them, "Go into all the world and proclaim the gospel to the whole creation."

MARK 16:15

The Spirit of the Lord is upon me, because he has anointed me to proclaim good news to the poor. He has sent me to proclaim liberty to the captives and recovering of sight to the blind, to set at liberty those who are oppressed, to proclaim the year of the Lord's favor.

LUKE 4:18-19

And I tell you, everyone who acknowledges me before men, the Son of Man also will acknowledge before the angels of God.

LUKE 12:8

He answered, "I tell you, if these were silent, the very stones would cry out."

LUKE 19:40

And that repentance for the forgiveness of sins should be proclaimed in his name to all nations, beginning from Jerusalem.

LUKE 24:47

How then will they call on him in whom they have not believed? And how are they to believe in him of whom they have never heard? And how are they to hear without someone preaching?

ROMANS 10:14

For if I preach the gospel, that gives me no ground for boasting. For necessity is laid upon me. Woe to me if I do not preach the gospel!

1 CORINTHIANS 9:16

But thanks be to God, who in Christ always leads us
in triumphal procession, and through us spreads the
fragrance of the knowledge of him everywhere.
2 CORINTHIANS 2:14

Since we have the same spirit of faith according to what
has been written, "I believed, and so I spoke," we also
believe, and so we also speak.
2 CORINTHIANS 4:13

Therefore, we are ambassadors for Christ, God making
his appeal through us. We implore you on behalf of
Christ, be reconciled to God.
2 CORINTHIANS 5:20

And [pray] also for me, that words may be given to me
in opening my mouth boldly to proclaim the mystery of
the gospel, for which I am an ambassador in chains, that
I may declare it boldly, as I ought to speak.
EPHESIANS 6:19-20

Him we proclaim, warning everyone and teaching
everyone with all wisdom, that we may present everyone
mature in Christ.
COLOSSIANS 1:28

Walk in wisdom toward outsiders, making the best use
of the time. Let your speech always be gracious, seasoned

with salt, so that you may know how you ought to answer each person.

COLOSSIANS 4:5-6

And I pray that the sharing of your faith may become effective for the full knowledge of every good thing that is in us for the sake of Christ.

PHILEMON 1:6

Through him then let us continually offer up a sacrifice of praise to God, that is, the fruit of lips that acknowledge his name.

HEBREWS 13:15

Is anyone among you suffering? Let him pray. Is anyone cheerful? Let him sing praise.

JAMES 5:13

But you are a chosen race, a royal priesthood, a holy nation, a people for his own possession, that you may proclaim the excellencies of him who called you out of darkness into his marvelous light.

1 PETER 2:9

16

A SIDEBAR
FOR INTROVERTS

Who has made man's mouth? . . . Is it not I, the Lord?
Now therefore go, and I will be with your mouth
and teach you what you shall speak.

EXODUS 4:11-12

IF YOU'RE AN INTROVERT, you may be wondering how all this "talk to people all the time in every situation" plays out. It's a fair question. It can be incredibly discouraging when we start to feel as though we must suppress our personality in order to be used by God. I don't think that's what he intends for us to feel. In fact, God gave each of us a unique personality on purpose, to reflect his image.

In all of this talk about engaging, I'm not suggesting that an introvert try to become an extrovert. Nor am I suggesting that introverts try to figure out how to become more talkative. I don't want to give you the impression that you should (in agony) force yourself to have conversations with people. This is not about being someone different from the person God designed you to be. In her book *Out of the Saltshaker and Into the World: Evangelism as a Way of Life*, Rebecca Manley Pippert says it like this: "Let God make you fully you. Rejoice in your God-given temperament and use it for God's purposes. This point cannot be emphasized enough. We must be authentic. If we try to be someone we are not, people will see it instantly."[1]

Now, all of this comes with a caveat: Walking in step with the Spirit will most certainly cause every one of us, regardless of personality type, to be stretched beyond our normal comfort zones. The Spirit will lead us to speak when we otherwise wouldn't and to say things we normally wouldn't say. We shouldn't stifle what God is doing just so we can remain "true to our personality." But we also shouldn't think we have to stifle our personality in order to be a part of what God is doing.

What I'm suggesting is that every believer (regardless of personality and other propensities) must learn how to live as a spiritual person. We all speak. We all communicate. We all have a sphere in which we operate day by day. As spiritual people, we should allow God to flow into our language regularly. If you're the type of person who gets by on a dozen words a day, let those dozen words be saturated with your love for God. If your word count is numbered in the thousands, let those thousands of words reflect your walk with Jesus. To whatever degree you speak, speak as a spiritual person.

My wife is an introvert. She loves God and lives out her faith in her interactions with other people. Her way of living out loud is quieter and gentler than my way of living out loud, but we both allow God to use us.

Jeanne goes to the grocery store several times a week (because in New York City you only buy what you can carry home). She tends to see the same cashiers again and again. Through her regular, kind greetings—a polite and sincere "How are you today?" is all it takes—she has turned those familiar faces into casual acquaintances.

There was a particular cashier named Maria with whom Jeanne had started feeling a rapport. She interacted with Maria over several months, always asking how her family was doing. Jeanne would share about our kids and how our son had moved far away but that she knew God was taking care of him. As Maria gradually opened up, Jeanne would tell her that God loves her and that, like Hagar in the Bible who had struggles, God sees her. Jeanne also let Maria know that she was praying for her.

One day, Jeanne was waiting in Maria's line with several customers in front of her. She could see that Maria was not her usual self. She scanned the groceries in a state of numbness, as if she were locking her emotions behind heavy doors in order to hold back a flood. With three customers still ahead of her, Jeanne locked eyes with Maria and gave a smile to say hello. Seeing the kind face of a friend was enough to break the dam of Maria's emotions, and she began to tear up. By the time Jeanne made it to the front of the line, Maria was openly crying as she shared that her son had just died of an overdose.

Right there, in the middle of a busy grocery store, Maria's line stopped moving. Hurried people slowed down to wait with patience, as if they knew something sacred was unfolding. Jeanne wept alongside Maria and prayed for her in the midst of her pain.

This moment was built on a foundation of steady interactions. Jeanne didn't have to say much in order to become a safe presence in Maria's life. Jeanne didn't have to act like an extrovert in order for God to be seen and heard in her life. She just needed to be herself and let God saturate her life and language.

INTROVERTED EVANGELIST

I asked my wife if she had some words of encouragement from one introvert to another. She has learned to navigate the call to engage people as an introvert, and I think she has some valuable insight into how God can use our personalities for his glory. Here is what she told me:

> Being an introvert may feel like a disability when you consider the idea of living out loud. I can share honestly from my personal experience and from coaching people with similar personalities that this is definitely not the case. I'm pretty sure I will never convince someone on the street to follow Jesus by debating theological points, but by his grace I have led others to Christ. It has been one of the greatest joys in my life, one that God has designed us all to experience.
>
> Believe it or not, there are some benefits to an introspective personality when it comes to living your faith openly. Introverts are sometimes more intentional in this regard. They often rely on the power of the Spirit because they may not feel they can rely on their own abilities. This is a strength disguised as a weakness. It's never bad to go into a situation aware of your need for God.
>
> In many cases, introverts also listen well. Those of us who aren't eager to talk tend to be good at listening. A very powerful part of engaging someone spiritually is demonstrating actual interest in that person as an individual.

Listening well shows love.

Introverts may perceive someone in need before an extrovert would. We take in the world around us a bit differently, and sometimes that means we will notice things that others wouldn't. Sharing words of hope and life in these situations, or asking, "Can I pray for you right now?" often impacts others powerfully and leads them to begin their journey of discovering God.

If spiritual engagement is something you have left to the extroverts, let me encourage you to step out in faith. Pray for very clear openings and even for others to approach you or initiate with you when you are just getting started. God has answered that prayer for me many times. Most important, know that awkwardness never prevents the Spirit from working; people respond to spiritual exchanges because God is drawing them, not because of a perfectly smooth social interaction. God uses each of us regardless of personality or gifts. It is his work from beginning to end.

A friend who read this manuscript during the development process offered his own perspective on what it looks like to live out loud as an introvert. If you're also an introvert, you may know where he's coming from.

Most introverts I know don't feel the need to hear themselves talk, so we quickly revert to active listening and processing while the extroverts do most of the talking. The important thing is being comfortable in your own skin.

One insight that I've found particularly helpful, and that pertains to living out loud as an introvert, is that everyone—introvert or extrovert—has a *preferred relational style*. Mine is "one-on-one" or "small group familiar." But even a small group can be too large at times. In fact, it just happened the other night at a new small group my wife and I have joined. Through the course of the evening with four other couples, my wife wasn't able to say much, but I made a few comments based on my own experience of the Christian faith that seemed to be well received. Afterward, one of the other men in the group (the kind of extrovert who is always saying to his wife, "Hey, honey, tell that story about . . .") said to me as we were walking out together, "Paul, you're an insightful guy. You should talk more." My reply was something along the lines of, "I try to speak up when I feel I have something to say."

Anyway, once a group grows to three or more, it's going to be tough for the introverts to get the floor. The great thing about one-on-one interactions is that it's just you and the other person. It can still be hard to get a word in edgewise sometimes, but there's a better chance when it's only one other person you're waiting on. I can stand up in front of dozens or hundreds of people and give a talk, but to really relate to people, I'm at my best one-on-one. So as I try to live out loud, those are the kinds of opportunities I can see myself gravitating toward.

When it comes to engaging people, God doesn't use extroverts more than introverts. I know many introverts who are more fruitful than many extroverts. In fact, I would go so far as to say that from what I read in Scripture, it seems more likely that Jesus was an introvert than an extrovert. He often looked for opportunities to be quiet and alone. He recharged by retreating to spend time with his Father whenever possible.

God is more interested in our *availability* and our *willingness* than he is in our temperament. He uses people who love him and who naturally live out who they are. When we align ourselves with God's heart to seek and save those who are lost, we can expect God to use us. When we walk in step with the Spirit, we can expect that he will open our mouths at the right times and in the right ways—regardless of whether it's our natural gifting to speak; regardless of what we think are our weaknesses; and definitely regardless of our mood at the moment. If we let him, he will use us, whether it's five words or a hundred words at a time.

17

SEEKING DAILY INTIMACY

The man who lives without faith in God
may be said to exist rather than to live,
and misses the true aim of his being.

H. W. WATKINS

I WILL NEVER FORGET a TV interview I once saw with Olympic figure skater Nancy Kerrigan's mother. She was sitting on the side of the rink with a TV monitor only inches from her face. She sat that close to the screen because she was legally blind. If she pushed her face right up to the monitor, she could just barely make out some blurry images.

The interviewer asked, "What can you see of your daughter?"

Nancy's mother said she could see a shadow moving around the ice, and she could tell when Nancy jumped. Then she began to tear up and said, "The thing that hurts, that I want so badly, is to see her face."[1]

There is something about seeing a person's face that draws us into a deeper connection. So much can be conveyed by an expression or through the eyes. It's why we avoid eye contact when we're saying or hearing something difficult. It's why the inability to make eye contact is often a sign of other problems. It's why it's considered impolite to stare. Eye contact is a form of intimacy.

One common lament we see throughout the Psalms is the agony of God hiding his face. David cries out again and again, "How long, O Lord, will you hide your face from me?"[2] Even though David wasn't actually looking into the eyes of God, God's face represents friendship, favor, and closeness. It was tragic for David when (because of his sin) that intimacy was lost. As he gropes for words deep enough to convey his pain, he settles on the image of God turning away his face. And he longs to have that connection restored.

Throughout Scripture, and also in the history of the church, the idea of seeing God's face has been linked to our closeness with him. We talk about turning our eyes to Jesus. We know that his presence is our joy. We hear about him turning his face toward—or away from—someone. We ask him to reveal himself to us. We want to look upon him. These are all ways to express a sense of intimacy.

Living out loud, at its core, is about a deep, intimate, heartfelt connection with God. "For out of the abundance of the heart his mouth speaks."[3] This passage suggests that we almost won't be able to conceal the things or people that have our hearts. And no matter how much we might intend to talk about God, it won't happen if our hearts are set on something other than him.

In his book *Evangelism as Exiles*, Elliot Clark says it powerfully:

Worship is essential to evangelism.

These days we tend to view preaching as something only preachers do. But preaching is really a close cousin to praise—and we praise things all the time. . . .

Peter tells us we've been set apart for this special service. We're called to declare God's praises to the world. So if we're not faithfully proclaiming the gospel to those around us, it's owing to the fact [that] we're not overflowing in praise to God. If evangelism doesn't exist, it's because worship doesn't.

Praise is the most natural thing in the world for us, and we do it all the time. We brag about our favorite sports team. We rave about restaurants. We shamelessly tell others about the deals we find online. We can't stop talking about the latest Netflix series or our last vacation. We adore musicians, endorse politicians, and fawn over celebrities. We promote our kids' school and post about our morning coffee. We sing the praises of just about everything, even gluten-free pizza.

But ask us to raise our voices in praise to God outside of weekend worship, and we struggle to string together a whole sentence. While we (and I include myself here) demonstrate an incredible ability to proclaim the glories of endless earthly trivialities, we somehow stutter and stammer at the opportunity to speak with others about our heavenly hope. So it's obvious our gospel silence isn't because our mouths are broken; it's because our hearts are. Because if we worshiped God as we should, our neighbors, coworkers, and friends would be the first to hear about it.[4]

Is God's faithfulness on the tip of your tongue? Does his goodness permeate your language? Are you eager to tell others what he is doing in your life, or how you are praying, or what Scripture you are reading? If these things never enter your conversations because they don't cross your mind, then it is time to evaluate what place Jesus has in your heart.

You will never be able to let your love for God flow into your everyday language unless you actually love God. People can tell when our words are a genuine expression of who we are, and when we're merely attempting to appear a certain way.

A few years ago, a friend of mine realized that a lot of guys he hung out with were interested in sports. Wanting to connect with his friends, he memorized a few current sports statistics. When the conversation came up, he inserted his stats in an effort to add to the conversation. The problem was that he had no real interest in the information he was spouting, no ability to follow up his stats with any useful information, and nowhere else to go in the conversation. And the other guys saw right through it. If my friend was going to have anything truly worth adding to the conversation, he needed to start by becoming genuinely interested in sports.

In the same way, whatever we say to others about God must be a genuine expression of who we are or else we won't have anything truly worthwhile to add to a spiritual conversation. If you don't feel confident that God has your heart, put this book down and start pursuing closeness with him. Search for him in the Scriptures. Talk to him in prayer. Ask him to open your eyes and soften your heart. Find someone to encourage you in your faith. Read, pray, seek. There is nothing more important than loving God with all your heart, soul, mind, and strength.[5]

HABITS

If you want to know what really has a hold on your heart, look at your habits. The rhythms that echo through your daily routines shape who you are. The things you do when you first wake up, the subconscious way you spend your lunch break, or the evening schedule you keep—all these patterns are forming you. They are perfectly designing your day to draw your attention toward something and away from something else. As Annie Dillard writes, "How we spend our days is, of course, how we spend our lives. What we do with this hour, and that one, is what we are doing."[6]

Intimacy with God is something we must cultivate. It is forged in the habits that make up our days, in the ideas that set the tone for our thoughts, in the decisions that drive our actions, and in the affections that orient our hearts. Seeing the face of God begins with *seeking* the face of God. "Anyone who comes to him must believe that he exists and that he rewards those who earnestly seek him."[7]

How do we go about seeking God? Though it might seem like an answer you've heard before, seeking God's face is about practicing the sorts of things that draw your attention to him—including reading and memorizing Scripture, praying, fasting, spending time with other believers, serving, giving, and breaking bread. All these habits of spiritual discipline promote intimacy. Donald S. Whitney, in his book *Spiritual Disciplines for the Christian Life*, reminds us to be people who seek God's face in this way:

> Think of the Spiritual Disciplines as ways we can place ourselves in the path of God's grace and seek Him. . . .
>
> The Spiritual Disciplines then are also like channels of God's transforming grace. As we place ourselves in them to seek communion with Christ, His grace flows to us and we are changed. . . .
>
> Tom Landry, coach of the Dallas Cowboys football team for most of three decades, said, "The job of a

football coach is to make men do what they don't want to do in order to achieve what they've always wanted to be." In much the same way, Christians are called to make themselves do something they would not naturally do—pursue the Spiritual Disciplines—in order to become what they've always wanted to be, that is, like Jesus Christ.[8]

I have come across many believers who say they want to *see* God's face but have never created habits of *seeking* God's face. Where we put our energy, what keeps our attention, what forms our patterns and dictates our actions, will have our hearts. And what is in our hearts will come out of our mouths.

INTIMACY LONGS FOR INTIMACY

A sure mark of someone who has intimacy with God is their continued desire for intimacy with God. Once we have tasted something delicious, we don't walk away thinking, *I'm glad I had that experience; now I never have to eat that scrumptious thing again.* No, we look forward to our next opportunity, because we have tasted and seen that it is good.[9] Intimacy with God has the same effect.

Writer Jon Bloom reflects on the life of Moses as evidence of this:

Has it ever struck you that Moses, from the depths of his being, pleaded with God, "Please show me your glory" (Exodus 33:18)? Bear in mind, he prayed *after* he had experienced unsurpassed theophanies: the burning bush, the signs in Egypt, the exodus and Red Sea deliverance, the pillar of cloud and fire, the miraculous provisions in the wilderness, the miraculous victory over the Amalekites, the Mount Sinai encounters, and God speaking to him in great detail all along the way.

If we could go back in time, we might be tempted to ask Moses, "It seems like God has shown you so much of his glory. What more do you want?" Moses, I think, would have been puzzled by the question and probably would have answered something like, *"More* of God's glory, of course. I've barely glimpsed 'the outskirts of his ways'" (Job 26:14). And he would have been right.[10]

Intimacy with God becomes the preoccupation of a heart that has intimacy with God. And living out loud is a natural byproduct. God's close and consistent presence in our lives turns us into evangelists by nature. Thoughts of him stir in us and invade our speech, and suddenly we find ourselves engaging with people spiritually through the overflow of our hearts.

Anyone can share the message of Jesus. Paul even talks about people who did it for evil reasons.[11] Evangelism is possible for anyone who knows the facts of the gospel. But living out loud is only possible for those who have intimacy with God. Living out loud is not sharing facts or performing a duty or manipulating crowds; living out loud is openly allowing others to see your love for God as it naturally bubbles up from your heart and out of your mouth. As Henry Martyn, an eighteenth-century missionary to India and Persia, once said, "The Spirit of Christ is the spirit of missions. The nearer we get to him the more intensely missionary we must become."[12]

A WORTHWHILE INVITATION

*Evangelism is the cure
to the disease of church boredom.*

TODD P. MCCOLLUM

JESUS AND HIS DISCIPLES had been walking for days. They were in the middle of a long journey and had made it to a stopping point. Jesus sat down by a well outside a city while his disciples went into town to grab some food. He was tired, "wearied . . . from his journey,"[1] according to John, and the sun was beating down in the heat of the day.

When a woman approached the well to draw water, there were a million reasons not to talk to her. This was supposed to be rest time for Jesus, both physically and emotionally. He was probably embarrassingly dirty and sweaty and possibly stinky—not exactly a great time to chat with a stranger. The woman was at the well during a time of day when no one else was around, so maybe she wasn't even interested in talking. She was most likely busy and not looking to be interrupted. She was from a different culture and religion, which could get in the way of a real connection. Plus any conversation between a man and a woman in that culture—or any culture—could be awkward in and of itself.

From a human standpoint, it would have been perfectly reasonable for Jesus to talk himself out of engaging her in that moment. But instead of finding reasons to avoid her and drifting off for a nap, Jesus struck up a conversation. He took the common experience of drinking water and turned it into a Shema statement about living water. He pressed in when she wanted to talk about spiritual things. He brought their conversation around to her need for a Savior, and the woman went away completely changed from their interaction.

Jesus often took normal, everyday life experiences and used them as an on-ramp to the gospel.

"See that temple? It's like my body."[2]

"Look at those sheep. They remind me of what it's like to follow God."[3]

"Hand me that mustard seed and let me tell you about the Kingdom of God."[4]

To follow Jesus and walk alongside him as a disciple was firsthand training in living out loud. Of course there were moments when the disciples stood boldly on street corners preaching the gospel to all who would listen. It's easy to read their stories and assume that it was all so epic; but I think there were many moments in between those big ones. Moments when they would glance over at a stone, or tear off a piece of bread, and strike up a conversation with someone as they remembered the way Jesus spoke to them in the everyday things of life.

Jesus didn't just tell us to make disciples of all nations; he showed us how. He walked around letting his love for God flow into his conversations. He loved God with all his heart, soul, and might, and he displayed it in everything he did. This is at the heart of what it means to be a Christian—yet, somehow, for so long, many of us have missed it.

DON'T SETTLE FOR BOREDOM

I was talking with a friend a while back. She has been a Christian for a long time but was battling some rebellion in her life. There were things that seemed more interesting and exciting than walking with Jesus, and she had gotten tangled up in them. As we were talking about how she'd gotten there and why she'd gone after those things, we stumbled onto something I think is true of so many believers: She was bored. Her walk with Jesus had become lackluster, and it didn't have the potency to stand up against the intrigue of worldly pursuits.

She had believed in a gospel that was really only about saving her from eternal damnation. That was where the gospel's relevance began and ended for her. She didn't realize that the gospel was an all-encompassing invitation to become a new person and live in a new type of relationship with God and other people. Or at least she didn't know how that went further than a morning Bible study and an occasional prayer.

When we spoke, she had already decided to step away from the sin (that's why we were having the conversation in the first place), but she really didn't know what to step into. So we talked about how Jesus has invited us to participate in his mission on earth and whether that was compelling enough for her to let go of the other stuff. We talked about how Jesus wants to turn us into fishers of men as we follow him. How he commissioned us to bring the gospel to the ends of the earth. And how he excitedly gave us his Spirit to enable us to do those things. As we talked, we realized that Jesus invites us into a life of living out loud.

She decided that a good first step would be to try to incorporate Shema statements into her next few conversations with people. It wasn't a monumental goal or an elaborate display of repentance. It was just a commitment to take a few steps toward what she thought could be a more irresistible walk with Jesus. And you know what happened? The next time I saw her, she was beaming as she told me about the conversations she'd had with people. No one came to faith through those initial conversations. She didn't get the opportunity to share the gospel with anyone. But through having Jesus on the tip of her tongue, the substance of her walk with him began to shift.

Week after week, she shared how fun it was to talk about Jesus with other people. How it made her actually *want* to be in the Word so she'd have something to say. How it had given her a desire to pray more frequently and more boldly. She also began to recognize the Spirit's presence in her life as she paid more attention to his promptings. And as she pursued this renewed walk with Jesus, the things that had been a distraction became less and less appealing. Now that the gospel had come alive to her, she realized she had something to lose by chasing after other things. Living out loud became an all-encompassing invitation to become a new person in Christ and live in a new type of relationship with God and with the people around her.

The church is full of people like my friend—people who have become bored with Christianity because they are living a version of faith that they built for themselves. A weak faith built on our own limited understanding, fueled by our whims and desires, is not compelling, and it doesn't stand up against the distractions, temptations, and promises of the world. Now more than ever, people are deconstructing their faith, buying into the culture's thoughts and agendas, and going after things that seem more interesting than their self-funded ideas about Christianity.

What could be more miserable as a Christian than trying to follow God and the world at the same time? Starting with such a shallow view of what it means to be a Christian, you end up not really getting what your flesh is lusting for, and certainly falling short of what your spirit longs for. You get the worst of both worlds.

C. S. Lewis said it like this:

> The terrible thing, the almost impossible thing, is to hand over your whole self—all your wishes and precautions— to Christ. But it is far easier than what we are all trying to do instead. For what we are trying to do is remain what we call "ourselves," to keep personal happiness as our great aim in life, and yet at the same time be "good." We are all trying to let our mind and heart go their own way—centered on money or pleasure or ambition—and hoping, in spite of this, to behave honestly and chastely and humbly. And that is exactly what Christ warned us you could not do."[5]

Of course it would be difficult and boring—and even unsustainable—to live in that type of relationship with God. But Jesus invites us to something far different from what some have reduced Christianity to. Earlier in the same discussion, Lewis explains,

> The Christian way is different: harder, and easier. Christ says, "Give me All. I don't want so much of your time and so much of your money and so much of your work: I want You. I have not come to torment your natural self, but to kill it. No half-measures are any good. . . . I will give you a new self instead. In fact, I will give you Myself: my own will shall become yours."[6]

Jesus wants us to walk with him, to know and hear him. He wants us to become like him and help others do the same. And let me just tell you: Living this way—living out loud—is *fun*. It's adventurous, courageous, freeing, and compelling. Living out loud isn't a new strategy for evangelism; it's a recapturing of that lost invitation. And it draws us into the only kind of Christian life worth living.

Maybe you recognize yourself in the words of C. S. Lewis. Maybe you always seem to be caught between the conviction that Jesus is the way, the truth, and the life, and the fleshly inclination that the world is more fun than following him. I want to encourage you with this: It is very likely that you have only scratched the surface of what a relationship with Christ can be. It makes sense that your heart would be pulled toward things that seem more interesting. But let me also encourage you that there is depth and vigor to a walk with Jesus that will captivate your heart and rivet your attention like nothing the world has to offer.

What keeps it fresh is the joy of seeing other people fall in love with Jesus. There's an excitement to the whole thing when it's brand new. There's a thrill to studying the Bible with someone who has never read it; showing people *hope* they've been waiting their whole life to find; and introducing people to a Jesus they've never met. These things bring it all back to the surface again and again for us. It's like going to a wedding after you've been married for ten years and feeling all the emotions rush back in. We weren't intended to be surrounded by people who have forgotten what it's like to encounter the living Jesus. We are meant to continually encounter people who are falling in love with him for the first time. And it's exhilarating when we do.

So while living out loud doesn't sum up everything it means to follow Jesus, and Shema statements are not, in and of themselves, the gospel, they are still a great place to start. In Matthew 22:35-37, when one of the Pharisees asks Jesus about the greatest commandment, Jesus responds by quoting the beginning of the Shema. I believe the Pharisees would have known that loving God with all our heart, soul, and might includes the very next part of the Shema:

> These words that I command you today shall be on your
> heart. You shall teach them diligently to your children,
> and shall talk of them when you sit in your house, and
> when you walk by the way, and when you lie down, and
> when you rise. You shall bind them as a sign on your
> hand, and they shall be as frontlets between your eyes.
> You shall write them on the doorposts of your house and
> on your gates.
> DEUTERONOMY 6:6-9

So next time you're talking with someone in your day-to-day life, remember that you are a new creation with the potential to change the conversation. Think about how you can let God be a part of the dialogue. Shift your perspective to see a waiting harvest, and ask the Holy Spirit to move your mouth. Try a Shema statement and see where it takes things. And as you learn to live out loud, see how speaking about God begins to reinvigorate your walk with him.

BRINGING SHEMA STATEMENTS
INTO YOUR DAILY LANGUAGE

BECAUSE EVERY SHEMA STATEMENT is based on *context*—the specific circumstances you're in, your personality and relational style, and the flow of the conversation—we can't give you a list of Shema statements that will always be appropriate. We've found that it is unproductive for people to memorize a list of Shema statements, because they come across as more of a strategy and result in unnatural interactions. That being said, many people have asked us *how* to bring Shema statements into their daily language. So it might be helpful to compare some non-Shema statements with possible Shema statements for the same situation. This may give more clarity to what we mean by Shema statements.

NON-SHEMA STATEMENT	SHEMA STATEMENT
I'm glad it all worked out.	I'm glad it all worked out. God has a way of making things happen.
That sunset is a work of art, isn't it?	Wow, that sunset is a work of art. God is quite an artist, isn't he?
I hope you feel better.	I'm going to pray that you get better quickly.
Wow, your home is beautiful.	God has blessed you with a beautiful home.
I need to be more patient.	The Holy Spirit is really convicting me that I need to grow in patience.
I feel very anxious about this virus.	I feel very anxious about this virus, but I'm trying to remember that God is in control.
I really want to help those who are homeless.	God is giving me a desire to do more to help the homeless.
I'm so happy about this opportunity.	I'm so thankful God has given me this opportunity.
I have a lot of resentment toward my sister. I guess I should try to forgive her.	I am struggling with resentment toward my sister. I know God is calling me to forgive her, but it's difficult, and I really need his help.
You did a great job on that project!	You did a great job on that project! God has given you a gift for working with numbers.

The statements in the left-hand column are all perfectly normal and appropriate. The statements in the right-hand column can also be perfectly normal and appropriate if they genuinely convey what you think. Start by learning to *recognize* God's hand in your daily life. Then when you're in conversation with someone, simply express what's on your mind. Though it may feel uncomfortable at first, it will begin to feel completely natural the more you express your spiritual thoughts.

NOTES

CHAPTER 1: A SHEMA LIFESTYLE
1. For more background on the Shema, see "The Shema," My Jewish Learning, accessed December 21, 2023, https://www.myjewishlearning .com/article/the-shema.
2. Mark 12:30.

CHAPTER 2: A NEW TYPE OF PERSON
1. Ephesians 4:22-24.
2. Matthew 5:13.
3. John R. W. Stott, *Christian Counter-Culture: The Message of the Sermon on the Mount* (Leicester, UK: Inter-Varsity Press, 1978), 65.
4. Albert Barnes, "Commentary on 2 Corinthians 2," *Barnes' Notes on the Whole Bible*, 1870, https://www.studylight.org/commentaries/eng/bnb /2-corinthians-2.html.
5. 2 Corinthians 2:15.
6. Matthew 5:14.
7. Matthew 5:14-15.
8. Glenn Stanton, "FactChecker: Misquoting Francis of Assisi," The Gospel Coalition, July 10, 2012, https://www.thegospelcoalition.org/article /factchecker-misquoting-francis-of-assisi/.
9. Duane Litfin, *Word versus Deed: Resetting the Scales to a Biblical Balance* (Wheaton, IL: Crossway, 2012), 12–13. Italics in the original.

CHAPTER 3: TODAY'S HARVEST

1. "Sharing Faith Is Increasingly Optional to Christians," Barna, modified May 15, 2018, https://www.barna.com/research/sharing-faith-increasingly -optional-christians/.
2. Luke 10:2.
3. John 5:17.
4. 2 Corinthians 5:20.
5. John 4:35, NIV.
6. Luke 19:10.
7. John 3:12; 1 Corinthians 15:40; 2 Corinthians 4:18; 5:2; Ephesians 1:20; 2:6; 3:10; 6:12.
8. John 21:6.
9. Hebrews 11:6.

CHAPTER 4: PRODIGAL FARMING

1. "Sonar," The Mariners' Museum and Park, accessed January 5, 2024, https://exploration.marinersmuseum.org/object/sonar/.
2. "Sonar"; James Dinneen, "Reginald Fessenden and the Invention of Sonar," *Distillations Magazine*, Science History Institute, May 19, 2020, https://sciencehistory.org/stories/magazine/reginald-fessenden-and-the -invention-of-sonar/.
3. Elliot Clark, *Evangelism as Exiles: Life on Mission as Strangers in Our Own Land* (n.p.: Gospel Coalition, 2019), 91.

CHAPTER 5: THE SPIRIT MOVES MOUTHS

1. Luke 19:40.
2. Dwight Lyman Moody, *New Sermons, Addresses, and Prayers* (Chicago: J. W. Goodspeed, 1877), 350.
3. Acts 6:15.
4. Acts 7:51, NIV.
5. James I. Packer, "The Work of the Holy Spirit in Conviction and Conversion," Lausanne Movement, accessed January 5, 2024, https://lausanne.org/content/the-work-of-the-holy-spirit-in-conviction-and -conversion.

CHAPTER 6: PRACTICALLY SPEAKING

1. "Getting to the Gospel: The Shema Statement," Nations Next Door, accessed January 5, 2024, https://www.nationsnextdoor.com/lead-the -nations/getting-to-the-gospel-the-shema-statement.

NOTES

CHAPTER 7: ONLY TIME WILL TELL
1. 1 Samuel 16:7.
2. Mark E. Dever, *The Gospel and Personal Evangelism* (Wheaton, IL: Crossway, 2007), 109.
3. Acts 9:15.

CHAPTER 8: DIVINE APPOINTMENTS
1. Jim Elliff, "A More Spontaneous and Genuine Evangelism," Christian Communicators Worldwide, November 13, 2023, https://www.ccwtoday .org/2005/04/a-more-spontaneous-and-genuine-evangelism. Italics in the original.
2. *Merriam-Webster*, s.v. "divine (*adj.*)," accessed January 5, 2024, https://www.merriam-webster.com/dictionary/divine.
3. *Merriam-Webster*, s.v. "appointment (*n.*)," accessed January 5, 2024, https://www.merriam-webster.com/dictionary/appointment.

CHAPTER 10: SELLING JESUS
1. Ron Marshall, "How Many Ads Do You See in One Day?," Red Crow Marketing, September 10, 2015, https://www.redcrowmarketing.com/2015 /09/10/many-ads-see-one-day/.
2. Matthew 16:24-26.
3. Timothy Keller (@timkellernyc), Twitter post, April 5, 2019, 1:33 p.m., https://twitter.com/timkellernyc/status/1114234499750141953.
4. John 8:11.
5. See, for example, Matthew 12:9-12; 21:23-27; Luke 14:1-34; 20:1-18.

CHAPTER 11: THE LAW OF THE FARM
1. "McCartney Live in Space," on Paul McCartney's official website, November 9, 2006, https://www.paulmccartney.com/news/mccartney -live-in-space.
2. The Paul McCartney Project, accessed January 5, 2024, https://www.the -paulmccartney-project.com/songs/.
3. Jim Elliff, "A More Spontaneous and Genuine Evangelism," Christian Communicators Worldwide, November 13, 2023, https://www.ccwtoday .org/2023/11/a-more-spontaneous-and-genuine-evangelism/.

CHAPTER 13: THE DOORWAY OF BROKENNESS
1. Matthew 11:28.
2. Psalm 107:4-6.

3. Mark 5:22-23.
4. Luke 10:8-9.

CHAPTER 14: CAVING IN TO CULTURE

1. Though some version of this quote is widely attributed to D. L. Moody, we were unable to ascertain a definitive source.
2. Gregory S. Berns et al., "Neurobiological Correlates of Social Conformity and Independence during Mental Rotation," *Biological Psychiatry* 58, no. 3 (August 1, 2005): 245–253, https://pubmed.ncbi.nlm.nih.gov/15978553.
3. Proverbs 29:5; Isaiah 51:7; John 12:42-43.
4. John Piper, "The Stampede of Secularism Will Not Stop Conversions," Desiring God (website), July 20, 2015, https://www.desiringgod .org/articles/the-stampede-of-secularism-will-not-stop-conversions.

CHAPTER 15: THE EVILS OF FRIENDSHIP EVANGELISM

1. 1 Thessalonians 5:16

CHAPTER 16: A SIDEBAR FOR INTROVERTS

1. Rebecca Manley Pippert, *Out of the Saltshaker and Into the World* (Downers Grove, IL: InterVarsity Press, 1999), 105.

CHAPTER 17: SEEKING DAILY INTIMACY

1. For more on this story, see Dave Anderson, "Sports of The Times; 'I Never Can See Her Face,'" *New York Times*, February 20, 1992, https://www.nytimes.com/1992/02/20/sports/sports-of-the-times -i-never-can-see-her-face.html.
2. See Psalm 13.
3. Luke 6:45.
4. Elliot Clark, *Evangelism as Exiles: Life on Mission as Strangers in Our Own Land* (n.p.: Gospel Coalition, 2019), 102–103.
5. Mark 12:30.
6. Annie Dillard, *The Writing Life* (New York: Harper & Row, 1989), 32.
7. Hebrews 11:6, NIV.
8. Donald S. Whitney, *Spiritual Disciplines for the Christian Life* (Colorado Springs: NavPress, 1991), 17–18.
9. Psalm 34:8.
10. Jon Bloom, "Intimacy Comes through Trembling: The Surprising Path to More of God," Desiring God (website), September 3, 2020, https:// www.desiringgod.org/articles/intimacy-comes-through-trembling. Italics in the original.

11. Philippians 1:15-18.
12. Quoted in Arthur Judson Brown, *The Why and How of Foreign Missions* (Philadelphia: American Baptist Publication Society, 1908), 257–258.

CHAPTER 18: A WORTHWHILE INVITATION
1. John 4:6.
2. John 2:18-19, 21, author's paraphrase.
3. John 10:1-18, author's paraphrase.
4. Luke 13:18-19, author's paraphrase.
5. C. S. Lewis, *Mere Christianity* (San Francisco: HarperSanFrancisco, 2001), 197–198.
6. Lewis, *Mere Christianity*, 196–197.

ABOUT THE AUTHORS

KEVIN KING is cofounder and president of International Project, a missions-sending organization focused on church planting among unreached people groups across the globe. International Project has a variety of teams in New York City, as well as in other cities in North America and internationally.

Kevin has a BA in Bible, an MA in biblical counseling, and an MDiv. His passion for evangelism began when he gave his life to Christ in high school—and later intensified to focus on reaching people who have never heard the gospel. He then discovered the strategic advantage of working with international students and the people groups God was bringing to the US through migration.

Kevin and his wife, Jeanne, moved to New York City in 1998 and began sharing the gospel on college campuses and in ethnically diverse neighborhoods. Through the people they've led to Christ, churches have been planted in multiple countries. In 2010, Kevin founded Equip, a ten-month program training cross-cultural church planters to start simple churches that will expand and multiply. A core element of the training is equipping Christians to live their faith out loud in everyday conversations. Workers from multiple missions agencies who have gone through the Equip training are now serving effectively around the world.

Kevin enjoys overseeing the International Project teams, as well as engaging in and starting Bible studies with international graduate students through Jeanne's ongoing campus ministry. He also loves running, scuba diving, and hiking. Kevin and Jeanne live in Harlem, where they raised their two children, who are now grown.

CHRISTINE DANIELS is a writer, content creator, and church planter with a passion for displaced people in desperate places. For more than fifteen years, across more than twenty countries, Christine has been documenting and telling stories of what God is doing around the world.

She is a coproducer and host of *The Maverick Podcast: Stories of People Who Dare to Go against the Grain*. An adventurer at heart, an overthinker by nature, and an extrovert by choice, Christine's life is an interesting mix of all things marvelous and mundane—which are just the sorts of things she likes to write about most. Although storytelling is her job, she believes the most important things in life happen off the record and out of the spotlight (and usually over a meal).

With a background in biblical studies, and a history of working in women's ministry, Christine loves to see marginalized women discover their identity in Christ. Today, she lives and works in the Middle East with her husband and two children.

INTERNATIONAL
PROJECT

International Project seeks to see the gospel established among unreached people groups. We believe God is divinely orchestrating migration, giving us an opportunity to reach the least reached in new ways. We are working to share the Good News with the nations by engaging the diaspora—those who have left their homelands for either refuge or opportunity. Through gospel sowing, discipleship, and church planting, we are seeing the message of Jesus spread to people groups and places that have been difficult to reach.

Alongside our long-term missionary teams in North America and Europe, International Project has short-term missions and training opportunities from one week to one year in length. We train people in how to *live out loud* and naturally engage others with the good news of Jesus. We seek to mobilize and equip the church in fruitful ministry in the harvest, specifically focused on the nations.

For more information, please check out internationalproject.org or contact us at info@internationalproject.org.

By purchasing
this book,
you're making
a difference.

For over 60 years, Tyndale has supported ministry

and humanitarian causes around the world through

the work of its foundation. Proceeds from every book sold

benefit the foundation's charitable giving. Thank you

for helping us meet the physical, spiritual, and

educational needs of people everywhere!

 Tyndale | Trusted. For Life.   **tyndale.com/foundation**

And don't forget to do good and to share with those in need. HEBREWS 13:16 (NLT)

CP1665